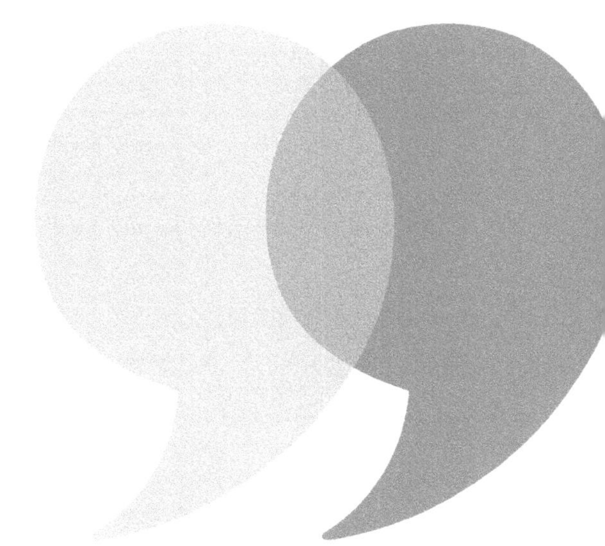

Remarkable Speaking

A Framework to Embody Your Voice and Your Vision

Shelley Goldstein

Remarkable Speaking
A Framework to Embody Your Voice and Your Vision

remarkablespeaking.com

Limits of liability and disclaimer of warranty

This book is strictly for informational and educational purposes only. The author and the publisher shall not be liable for any misuse of the enclosed material. The author and the publisher do not guarantee that anyone following these techniques, suggestions, tips, ideas, or strategies will be successful. The author and the publisher shall have neither liability nor responsibility to anyone with respect to any loss or damage caused, or alleged to be caused, directly or indirectly, by the information or suggestions contained in this book.

Published by Made to Change the World™ Publishing
Nashville, TN

Cover and interior design by Chelsea Jewell and Lorie DeWorken
Graphics by Elizabeth Baldwin
Illustrations by EB Keehn
Author photographs by Leslie Barton

ISBN: 978-1-956837-41-4 Paperback
978-1-956837-42-1 eBook

Printed in the USA, Canada, Australia, and Europe

This book is for you:

The leader with a message.
The visionary with a story to be told.
The remarkable speaker who is ready to
embody your voice and your vision equally.

CONTENTS

ACKNOWLEDGMENTS

Something unexpected happened when I was coaching clients. After the sessions ended, I'd hear comments like, "You gotta write this stuff in a book!" Honestly, I didn't think much of it, just a kind way of saying "Thanks, coach." But then clients started quoting me as their personal mantra. And then came "I want to speak like you" and "I hear your voice in the back of my head when I present"—I will never forget how I felt in those moments. They are what influenced me to write this book, and for that, *I thank you.*

I am forever grateful to my friends, mentors, and advisors, a community of cherished individuals, who guided me on this journey. Your unwavering support is a testament to the incredible encouragement and countless small acts of kindness that have made this book a reality. You've been my cheerleaders, confidantes, and partners in this creative endeavor. Your presence in my life has made all the difference. From the bottom of my heart, thank you for helping me amplify my voice.

To my parents for your unconditional love and championing me to pursue my vision no matter how unconventional. You taught me acceptance, patience, and what it means to enjoy life. I love you.

To my sister, Carolyn, and Jett, Anna, and Kitt: Thank you for giving me space to dream big.

My deepest gratitude to all of you in the Edelson family tree who listened.

To Gary for stepping up when I felt like I was falling down.

There are many to whom I express my utmost appreciation for sharing their expertise and their knowledge. Their contributions, both big and small, helped me bring my vision to life.

I thank Ellie Shefi for your dynamic leadership, directing me to where I am today.

Michael Gendler and Tristan de Montebello for adding joy to 2020 with Presenting in Pajama Pants, inviting me to get certified as an Ultraspeaking coach, and supporting my vision beyond the fundamentals of public speaking.

Benjamin Lee and Mark Bossert, the best partner-coaches anyone could ask for, who advocated for my journey to Remarkable Speaking.

Ella Cojocaru, John Sahakian, Grace Huang, and Roger Nolan for your teachings on breathwork and meditation that keep me ever present.

I am grateful to Fozzie Bear, Nera, Milton, Morrissey, Chaos, Echo, Gobi, Chloe, and Sam for constant companionship.

I admire and I thank Malala Yousafzai, Ruth Bader Ginsburg, Sebastião Salgado, Jane Goodall, Steve Hartman, Amanda Gorman, Judy Chicago, Diane von Furstenberg, and Diana, Princess of Wales, for speaking out when others could not.

Thank you to those whose quotes energized many conversations: William Ernest Henley, Lizzie Magie, Adam Schmalholz, Cher, Ken Burns, Louisa May Alcott, and Jonathan Gold.

Thank you Seth Godin, Simon Sinek, Michelle Obama, Adam Grant, Shelley Zalis, Rich Litvin, and Oprah Winfrey for your inspiring insights.

Special thanks to my editors, Megan Lowes and Stephanie Browning, and my book designers, Chelsea Jewell and Lorie DeWorken, for your guidance in making my words flow.

To the Remarkable Speaking marketing team for managing my digital stage.

Elizabeth Baldwin for designing graphics and a logo that transcends the purpose of my brand. EB Keehn for your illustrations that speak a thousand words. Leslie Barton for taking photographs that capture my essence.

For motivating my creative spark, I thank Theoni V. Aldredge, René Gruau, Arthur Bocce, Gary Brouwer, and Camille Claudel. Thanks to Daniel Geoly, Mr. Ludecker, Mitchell Rodbell, Niki Livas, and Joy Sures for giving me a chance because I danced to a different beat.

And to Marian Goodman for her encouragement to five-year-old Shelley, "To an especially creative little girl whom I know will someday become a beautiful dancer."

INTRODUCTION

My boss, "Ian," and I had arrived at the National Fitness Trade Show to help our client, "Buddy," market his newly-patented jump rope. But Buddy, the main presenter of the new product, was unexpectedly detained at the last minute. As the marketing director, I had intimate knowledge of the jump rope having planned the roll out over the last six months. So Ian handed me the rope and volunteered *me* to speak in Buddy's place.

I knew the material, but I wasn't prepared to give a formal presentation—I had no rehearsal, no notes, and no time to think! Looking at the audience, all eyes were on me. Paralyzed with fear, I was sure they knew I wasn't supposed to be the one presenting.

Taking a few deep breaths, my grip loosened on the jump rope in my sweaty hands. My eyes connected with a woman in the audience who was grinning, and at that moment, I handed her the rope. She was fascinated, eager to hear what I had to say. Then I turned to my boss and asked him to hand out our stock of ropes to more people. Before I knew it, the crowd was jumping in unison.

I felt strangely confident and less fearful as the presentation turned into an engaging shared experience.

You see, I didn't step into the speaker role because I had internal confidence or particular oratory skills. I embraced the speaker mantle because of something that happened externally—the encouraging reactions from the audience.

And that is when I started to believe. I learned that what I had to say externally was more important than the limitations I was putting on myself internally. It was audiences filled with people like you, and your encouraging reactions, that inspired me to write this book.

As you start to walk on the way, the way appears.

—Rumi

Maybe you feel comfortable speaking to friends but less comfortable speaking to large groups. Maybe you've avoided speaking professionally but want to know how to connect better with your colleagues. Maybe you've been speaking for a long time but are looking to improve your skills.

I hear you.

One of the greatest challenges for many leaders is the loneliness and isolation you experience at the top—visions of standing atop an ivory tower feeling intense pressure to speak. But the truth is you have the power to connect with countless numbers of people, and as you develop new skills through this book, you will learn to lead from your heart instead of from your head.

I feel you.

The journey to becoming a confident speaker can seem daunting. I should know; I've been there, struggling between self-doubt and fear. But within these pages you'll find the very same drills and framework that I have used, and still use to this day, to speak up and to use my voice.

I get you.

The training in these pages is going to be empowering and transforming. From the first chapter to the last, you'll learn skills that will improve your speaking through opportunities to speak everywhere. The book is filled with drills that guide you on how to find those speaking opportunities in real-world situations. By working in incremental steps, you'll have the time and space to reinforce what you learn and avoid becoming overwhelmed. In Chapter 7, you will use my time-saving framework to structure an entire speech in minutes! And by Chapter 10, you will have embodied what it means to be a remarkable speaker.

Throughout the book, I share what's worked for me and for my clients. You'll read about their real-life experiences as well as mine. If some of these stories resonate, you're in the right place.

When you take this approach to speaking, you will find your voice in the workplace and in all areas of your life. I want you to take a moment and visualize that idea ... in the workplace and in life. What is something you dread doing will become something you get excited about doing—and with much greater purpose!

My hope for you is that after reading this book you enjoy speaking as much as I do and experience what it means to be a remarkable speaker. But know this: Your experience is also a gift to me because my purpose as a coach is to raise the voice of every person, especially the unspoken. I believe when you speak up, you have an opportunity to change the world.

There's nothing that means more to me than creating a gateway for people to find their place in the world by helping them find their confidence. *Remarkable Speaking* is your gateway to confidence to speak what's on your mind in the way that you want and in your own words!

I am excited for what's to come for you because there's something brewing internally, and that is why you are here.

I am Shelley, your public speaking coach.

Welcome to *Remarkable Speaking*.

CHAPTER 1
REFRAME

To Be Remarkable, You Need to Embody

You're a high-performing entrepreneur, C-suite executive, president, or vice-president. You are remarkable at what you do because you have embodied your vision and continually strive for excellence. You know how to get what you want in life. You are confident and believe in your ability to succeed.

Yet you don't feel that way when you speak. So you're here to learn how to apply confidence and belief to your speaking and take your skills to the next level. The good news is that speaking remarkably is a skill you can learn and master.

As a speaking coach, it is important to me that every voice feels heard. As a speaker, it is important to me that every talk feels like I am sharing information through conversation. I'm inviting you to join me in a conversation for the next ten chapters to learn how to move the world with your words.

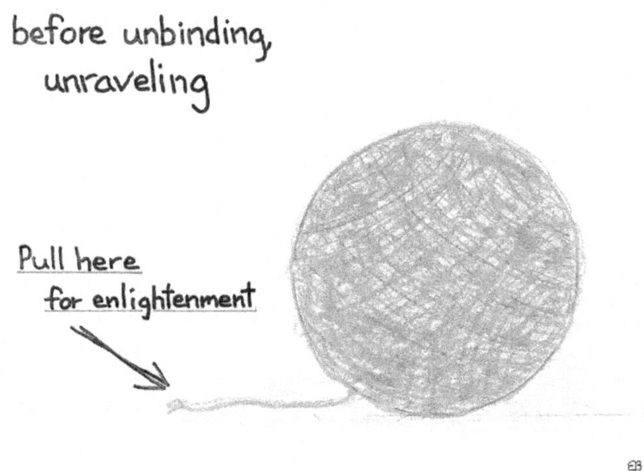

I wrote this book for action-driven leaders like you who can't afford to lose time or opportunities. Every chapter is divided into subchapters—each an important step on your journey to becoming a remarkable speaker. Through my process, the Remarkable Framework, I'll show you how to develop your speaking skills with drills (some of which may feel silly) that take only a few minutes. The Remarkable Framework, described as "life-changing" by my clients, will deliver results. And it is designed to fit into your life the way you live it.

You've likely been relying on the same tactics for a long time, and your confidence and speaking abilities haven't grown. So I am asking you to try something different. You can implement each step in the Remarkable Framework as quickly as you finish reading a given subchapter to experience real-life progress. That is how my clients built their routines and mastered the skill of speaking.

The purpose of this book is to teach you how to develop actual confidence when speaking, not just fake it. Sure, I could give you tricks and cheat sheets on how to speak like you have confidence, but there's a risk you'll talk in sound bites and sound just like everyone else. Instead, you'll learn to apply the Remarkable Framework to your entire life, as you live it, and elevate your voice in your own words.

Through this Framework, you will learn to speak authentically, draw on experience and emotion, and truly connect with your audience. Yes, it will also help you prepare for your talks but without fooling you into thinking that excessive preparation alone is the goal. Most people overly focus on preparation. While you can rehearse over and over, every situation is different, and you can't prepare for the unexpected. Think of how public speaking shows up in your life. It's not just in the boardroom or the next presentation. It's not just with family and friends. It's not just on the stage. Speaking happens everywhere.

I've coached a lot of professionals just like you. Having taken the journey you are about to take in this book, they now speak with an executive presence and stand out as visionaries who empower others. Following the Remarkable Framework, you too will get more of what you want out of your public speaking and your leadership.

The Remarkable Framework will become your public speaking solution. Within the Framework, I've included all of the drills, videos, and pro tips you need to improve your speaking skills. Additionally, I've compiled the worksheets for structuring any speech into a workbook that augments the chapters in this book. Now is a good time to scan the QR code on the book cover or go to remarkableframework.com to download your free workbook.

Remarkable Speaking is not a one-and-done process. The Remarkable Framework within this book is evergreen. You can rely on it whenever you feel nervous or unsure of what to say in any type of speaking situation. It will feel like I'm right there coaching you.

Remarkable Speaking is about embodying your voice and your vision equally. As a world-class leader, you will elevate your ability to be fully seen and speak beyond the scope of what you think is possible. Let your journey to discovering your authentic voice begin.

Get Out of Your Head

Picture it …
A clown, in full regalia, painted face, yellow hair, and floppy, oversized red shoes came running toward me during the busy lunch hour in midtown Manhattan. "Hey, Shelley, what time will I see you tonight?"

Maybe you're making a judgment about me right now. The scene was out of the ordinary, even by New York City standards.

The facts are that Ringling Bros. and Barnum & Bailey Circus was an important part of my journey. It was my first job as a costume designer with designer status and the beginning of many more opportunities. Charging down the street right out of clown alley (the backstage area in the circus), my colleague, the clown, was confirming the production meeting that was scheduled right before the show's opening night at Madison Square Garden.

Are you still making judgments about me?

Do you judge yourself before you know all the facts?

There's evidence to suggest that your brain predicts and makes assumptions up to ten seconds before you consciously make a decision.[1] If that is the case, then your self-talk may not be accurate. Ruminating and allowing your negative thoughts to dominate prevents you from sharing your experiences, and that's a disservice to those around you. More than you think, your audience wants to learn from your gems of knowledge. In that context, keeping valuable thoughts to yourself is selfish.

Consider that one person in the meeting who always hogs the conversion. Would you listen to them simply because they are more vocal than others, or would you tune them out because they come across as selfish? If you'd tune them out for appearing selfish, why would you not tune out your own bossy self-talk and let your experiences become the conversation?

Get out of your head and into the room.

Tuning out self-talk is like trying to tune out an earworm from a song that repeats in your head over and over again. Remember the song "Hey Ya!" by OutKast? When it first came out, the tune was on auto loop in my head for weeks. It played on every meme on social media; I heard it whenever I went to the gym and even in stores when I was shopping. "Hey Ya!" was all I could hear until, ironically, the song "It's My Life" by No Doubt hit the charts and replaced one annoying earworm with a completely different tune.

How do you change the self-talk in your head about public speaking? Like an earworm, replace one thought with another thought by reframing it. Stop thinking about how you feel about what you have to do as a leader, and reframe your self-talk to how you can help others. Instead of telling yourself not to speak up because people will judge every word you say, reframe that thought by turning the focus toward what others are doing. For example, highlight the junior designer's new widget that organizes device charging cables so they don't get tangled into a mess. You can relax because you're not hyper focused on how you appear, and, bonus, you're building an employee's confidence, bolstering their performance and happiness within your organization.

The world is so much bigger than your insecurities
And they don't speak on your behalf
Without your soul's authority

—IN-Q

The first step to speaking remarkably is to reframe your thoughts and turn the focus from you to the people you're speaking to. What do they need to hear at that moment? What problems have they encountered? What have you experienced that you can share as a valuable solution? Your audience is there to hear the answers to those questions. They want you to share your knowledge.

> **PRO TIP:** When you have a negative thought, consider different perspectives on the situation.

When you share your knowledge, people usually respond with, "I love what you said" and "I appreciate you letting me know." That's gold right there. You need no more confirmation that you are the subject-matter expert. Your listeners are the barometer of your success because their reactions will supersede any negative thought stuck in your head.

A mind is like a parachute.
It doesn't work if it is not open.

—Frank Zappa

Remember: You got the job. You got the title. Disconnect from what your judgment tells you to believe and embody what others actually believe about you.

That belief is what gives you confidence. Following are drills to strengthen your confidence, but there's an unexpected twist on how it's done. Read on to find out what it is.

Tongue Twisting Confidence Made a King

You may label yourself as an introvert or extrovert, maybe even an ambivert. Regardless, you may not feel like you're in control of your speaking or feel very confident about it.

I am a social butterfly. I have a bold personality, and people consider me an extrovert. Even so, I've been lost for words before an audience. I once had to present to stakeholders and council members for an environmental research project when the video portion of my slide deck would not play.

My adrenaline spiked like a geyser. I had prepared for weeks in many flawless rehearsals, but my brain, which had been buzzing with ideas, went as blank as a whiteboard.

I started fidgeting with video reset buttons. My fidgeting went to shaking. I tried to open my mouth to speak but stood tongue-tied blocking the screen. Everyone was intently watching me, waiting in anticipation.

I finally got the video to launch and finished my presentation, but from that traumatizing moment forward, stage fright kept me comfortably behind the scenes. I passed opportunities to speak up because fear of failure held me back. Despite all the preparation, I no longer trusted myself, and my self-talk took on the narrative of protecting me from looking foolish and being judged.

I also had confidence envy. I compared myself to my peers and colleagues who got the accolades and the big projects. They did a lot of the talking in meetings with an abundant level of self-assuredness. While I was ruminating about the risks of failing, their confidence seemed to get them more attention, which led to more of their successes and rewards.

While they enjoyed the spotlight, I slowly realized my selfish self-talk had been affirming my doubts and giving me reason to envy others. I came to learn that feeling confident has less to do with personality labels and more to do with what I know. When I doubt myself less, I can access confidence on demand by believing in what I know.

In 1926, an Australian speech and language therapist, Lionel George Logue, famously coached Prince Albert, the duke of York. While executing his royal responsibilities, the duke, who later would be crowned King George VI, would get tongue-tied and speak with a terrible stammer.

As silly as it may sound, Logue had the duke practice tongue twisters before he made his speeches. This daily routine helped the duke to relax when he spoke and gain confidence. Tongue twisters not only helped the duke to improve his pronunciation and confidence, they also helped him to focus. Because Logue had the duke concentrating on pronouncing the nonsense words quickly and repeatedly, there was little time for the duke to overthink and deliberate their association. Eventually, the duke barely stuttered a word.

If tongue twisters helped an eventual king to communicate with conviction, this drill I'm about to ask you to do can help you too. I am going to give you one instruction, that's all. Any other self-talk isn't part of the drill. It's merely an obstacle that you're pondering, distracting you while you're speaking. Focus on the one instruction to get into flow.

Sing like no one is listening, love like you've never been hurt, dance like no one is watching, and live like it is heaven on earth.

—Unknown

Repeat the following tongue twister until you can pronounce each word without fumbling. Because this is a speaking drill, say it out loud:

The thirty-three thieves thrilled the throne with thistles through Thursday.

PRO TIP: Focus on a clear pronunciation at a slower pace before increasing your speed. Once you can say it correctly slowly, gradually pick up the pace.

It may take you a few rounds, but stick with it. Once you get it, you will experience the feeling of executive presence.

Now I want you to repeat a ridiculous word—"bumfuzzle"—two times. Say what?! "Say What?!" is, in fact, what I call this drill. The first time, speak the word with commanding force as if it's the most important thing you have to say. The second time, speak the word with doubt as if you question what you're saying.

1. Commanding force: **Bumfuzzle!**
2. Doubt: *Bumfuzzle?*

PRO TIP: To speak with commanding force is to have strong intent as if you're pounding really hard on a drum. To speak with doubt is to have a shaky feeling as if you are walking on a tightrope thirty feet above the ground.

Notice the contrast. Think about the two styles of speaking; how would you describe your feeling each time? Which style felt more empowering? Which one left room for uncertainty? The commanding force is what confidence feels like. There's no doubting it when you say **"Bumfuzzle!"**

You can also feel confident even when not knowing, but not from doubt or ambivalence. Rather, when you admit that you don't know something, it shows that you're considering different perspectives and not jumping to rash conclusions. You're thoughtfully weighing the what-ifs as an opportunity to discover something new and trust your gut in your decision making.

People trust you more when you're honest and own up to the fact that you don't know something. Confidence has everything to do with both knowing your stuff as a subject-matter expert in your field *and* knowing your limitations. When you second guess yourself, you discredit yourself.

If you're having second thoughts when you present because you don't trust what you're saying, you're most likely speaking from the processing part of your brain—the frontal lobe. Your frontal lobe serves many functions that have to do with thinking and conscious activities, such as reasoning, processing information, and learning. It also helps you to focus your attention, direct movements like lifting your hand to scratch an itch, and figure out what to say.

So imagine your brain trying to do all those functions during a presentation. No wonder your speech stammers and you ramble with endless digressions. While critical thinking and reasoning are excellent skills, when you force your frontal lobe to do all that processing while you're speaking, it can't decipher what to say and break down complex thoughts simultaneously.

The temporal lobe, however, is where you use your senses and stored memories to communicate. The connection between these functions helps you to comprehend the meaning of words, form sentences, and experience emotions.

Tongue twister drills, thus, free up your frontal lobe from hyper processing so you can access the temporal lobe to recall everything you've stored in it, like memories and feelings derived from your senses (i.e., what you "know"). Whether reminiscing with friends or addressing a team or a boardroom of executives, the conversation flows when you tap into your memories rather than overtaxing your brain functions on the spot. You have lived and learned and earned your experiences, so it is natural for you to speak about them confidently. Like replacing negative thoughts with positive ones, reframing a speech as a conversation also offers a different perspective on how you see things, which will serve you as a confident speaker.

Start practicing tongue twisters daily to build your confidence. If you haven't done so yet, scan the QR code on the book cover or go to remarkableframework.com to download the workbook. For more tongue twister drills, refer to the Tongue Twisters section in the workbook. The drills take only a few minutes, but the difference will be palpable.

Curiosity Killed the Cat

Reframing your thoughts so you don't overthink is one way to gain confidence. Another way is by being curious.

This might remind you of the idiom, "curiosity killed the cat." It warns you that nosing around in someone else's business may get you into trouble. But in the second part of the idiom, satisfaction brought the cat back. Curiosity does not actually kill the cat because a cat has nine lives. The cat found satisfaction by asking questions and discovering new gems of information. It was worth the risk to be curious to feel happy.

Happiness comes from the adrenaline rush you get when you discover and experience something new. Dopamine, also known as the happy hormone, is released and acts as a chemical messenger in the brain motivating you to seek more satisfying and enjoyable experiences.

According to current MRI studies of the brain, psychologists are learning that curiosity also releases dopamine and boosts the hippocampus part of the brain, which reinforces your memory.[2] So, basically, asking questions of others, in more ways than one, is a great exercise for remarkable speaking. The more curious you are, the better you feel and the better things stick. When you show an interest in others by asking questions, you turn the focus away from you; you boost your brain's ability to help you feel happy, which, in turn, makes you feel confident; and you allow your audience to feel heard.

> To be interesting, be interested. Ask questions that other persons will enjoy answering.
>
> —Dale Carnegie

Radio host Larry King conducted over fifty thousand interviews in his career. Before his interviews, the king of talk radio would look over a few quick notes, but, for the most part, he didn't actually "prepare" for the interviews in too much detail. He said he always wanted to ask questions that he doesn't know the answer to. Rather than conducting an interview as an expert, King came to it to learn.

Similarly, pioneering TV news anchor and journalist Barbara Walters said, "It's not the first question, it's the follow up. 'What did you mean by that? Why do you say that?'"

You may have prepared an agenda for an interview or presentation with the expectation that that's what your audience wants to hear. There's nothing wrong with having a prepared agenda, but if your audience does not relate to your agenda or is unresponsive to your questions, they will not be very engaged with the conversation. Your expectation can lead to disappointment.

I have experienced disappointment while being interviewed on podcasts. I was looking forward to one particular podcast because the host and I were both public speaking coaches. I was excited to discuss our different approaches, but the host stuck to template Q&A.

They asked how I got started in my career, and I answered with my clown story in Midtown Manhattan. They responded: "Wow, that's great," then immediately followed with a question about what tips I had for the audience on confidence. I have plenty of tips, but they don't tell my story, and I didn't feel heard. How piqued is your curiosity reading about my work at the Greatest Show on Earth?

The tables were turned when I was the one conducting interviews for new hires. It only took a few candidates for me to figure out that the questions on my agenda weren't helping me get to know these people. The fourth candidate, "Fanny," was very soft spoken, and when I got more curious and really listened to her answers, she became more comfortable revealing her special interests. Those special interests involved skills that were not within the scope of the job description but were needed in other areas of my department. I adjusted the job description and hired Fanny. Not having expectations was the beginning of a very satisfying eleven-year professional relationship.

Many clients come to me for coaching specifically to host a podcast or for job interviews. I now share that curiosity is an opportunity to look past your expectations of the person or situation in front of you because what you find on the other side of your agenda is usually an engaging conversation where creativity and new relationships thrive.

Whether that relationship is between a leader and their team, a public speaker and their audience, or a podcast host and their guest, you can turn a disappointing situation into a satisfying one by asking more questions. In his book *Shift Your Mind Shift the World*,[3] coach and author Steve Chandler writes that most professional and personal relationships are based on expectations or agreements.

Expectations, he explains, are putting all the responsibility of a situation on someone other than you. Say you have an expectation for your team to deliver a prototype that you need for a client presentation by the tenth of the month, and they miss the deadline. You're frustrated because delays will increase costs with expedited shipping, and you don't have time to approve the prototype because you are flying out of town the next day to attend a conference.

But the team lead shares news that they have discovered a better mechanism for the product to operate more efficiently. While you might initially feel like expressing your dismay about the missed deadline, you instead ask more questions about the discovery, and you find out that the product can be made from locally sourced materials and will save two dollars per unit in production costs.

Instead of responding with frustration, you proudly tell the team that you're impressed with their discovery and appreciate their efforts to improve production. Feeling pride, the team is motivated to work late that night to finish the prototype and create a video to send to you for your approval before your conference starts. Everyone *agrees* this is a workable solution.

> Two voices cannot be perceived in one ear.
>
> —The Talmud

Chandler points out that people tend to honor agreements more than they live up to expectations. When you have a better understanding and more information about a situation, everyone involved can take responsibility for their role in the situation with a new agreement on moving forward.

To get an agreement from your audience when speaking, make it about them. Read the room to see if people are fidgeting with their phones and make eye contact to create a connection. If they are shaking their heads or sighing in agreement, acknowledge their responses and expand on that point. It can be as simple as asking a yes or no question.

When you're willing to be flexible with your agenda and show interest in your audience's needs, they'll have a greater appreciation of what you're talking about. It will be memorable, and you'll feel pretty confident—and that makes it a great experience for you and your audience.

The smartest person in the room is not necessarily the one with the answers, but rather the one asking the questions. The next time your confidence is waning, be a little curious.

If You Don't Do It, It Doesn't Work

You want to be a remarkable speaker for a reason—excellent speaking skills are an essential, if not the most important, part of business.

Warren Buffet had similar advice for a group of young professionals. "If you can't communicate, it's like winking at a girl in the dark—nothing happens. You can have all the brainpower in the world, but you have to be able to transmit it. And the transmission is communication."

You want your teams to be good at presenting, negotiating, networking, selling, giving feedback, onboarding, and all the many other ways there are to be productive. But just imagine if people were hired based on their speaking skills. There would be very few people working for the organization! Yet there's an expectation that everyone shows up in that way.

Invest in your speaking skills in the same way you might build a business or launch a new product. Your skills are your competitive advantage for building stronger relationships, experiencing unrealized growth of your personal brand, and collaborating more efficiently, expanding your market share. Excellent speaking skills increase your value because there's always another conversation to be had, another business to run, and another product waiting to be discovered.

Companies are built by people, run by people, and serve people. The Remarkable Framework is your opportunity to set a gold standard in creating a space where you can inspire employees to speak up, share their ideas, and impact their career journeys. When people feel like they're part of something bigger than themselves, companies grow.

But if you don't do the drills, the Framework doesn't work. It requires a solid commitment to the drills and no half-assing to take you further than you imagined.

When you're learning something for the first time, it may feel uncomfortable, even frustrating.

Learning a new habit, like reframing your thoughts, involves taking a different approach. Imagine each year of your life is like a layer of an onion. It took you hours, months, even years to develop your habits and build your knowledge base. When you're learning something new, you're unlearning something else, carefully peeling away one layer of the onion at a time to make room for a new layer to form. Give yourself the grace and compassion you need to rebuild those layers and learn new skills.

Your selfish self-talk may creep its way into your head and hold you back from time to time while you are on your journey of unlearning. When you tell yourself, "I'm not doing it right" or "I didn't say it the best way," reframe your focus on the things that you are doing well. Do more of what you are doing well, incrementally, subchapter by subchapter. That is how you'll improve.

Don't look for the big, quick improvement.
Seek the small improvement one day at a time.
That's the only way it happens—and when it happens, it lasts.

—John Wooden

Reading this book alone will not advance you to speaking excellence. That would be like reading a book to learn how to ride a bicycle. You'll learn a lot about the benefits of riding and the mechanics of how the gears work, but when you get on an actual bicycle, it will feel completely different. You will wobble and you will fall. Learning how to balance on a bicycle is a physical encounter that you cannot experience unless you actually get on the bike.

Every time you take a spin on that bicycle, you're creating new neural pathways in your brain. These pathways are formed by neurons firing together. Repetition is the key to strengthening the neural pathways and turning your behaviors into habits.

To embody the habit of speaking, you need to activate the Framework. Do the drills I suggest in this book, and do them a lot and often. The process can take as long as the time you put into it.

Some people follow former Harvard business professor Clayton Christensen's One Hundred Percent Rule: "It's easier to hold to your principles 100 percent of the time than it is to hold to them 98 percent of the time."[4]

Imagine a new product launch. You're not one hundred percent sold on the marketing campaign. There's something in the messaging that doesn't quite add up for you. So you're ninety-eight percent sold; according to Christensen, that's the same as no commitment at all. That two percent is enough uncertainty to mess with the team's confidence, and without one hundred percent buy-in, people start to see faults in the artwork and maybe the product itself. The morale behind the launch has been diluted, and everyone is feeling *sort of* excited.

Author and speaker Malcolm Gladwell professes it takes ten thousand hours to reach mastery in his book *Outliers*.[5]

Psychologist and researcher Phillippa Lally and her colleagues from University College London observed it takes anywhere from 66 to 254 days for a skill to be fully formed.[6]

Atomic Habits author James Clear wants you to "Just shut up and put your reps in!"[7]

Everyone has a different path to achieving public speaking excellence. At one meeting, you may feel really confident, and at the next speech, you may speak a little too fast, but you know you're making progress because of how people respond to you.

Every path to success has its own series of twists and turns, but there's always a path forward, one incremental step at a time. And with each rep that you practice, you're strengthening your confidence.

Legendary cellist Pablo Casals had a vigorous practice at age ninety. When people asked him why he continued to practice, he replied, "Because I think I'm making progress."

Whatever path you choose, there are opportunities in plain sight for you to speak remarkably everyday. In Chapter 2, I'll introduce you to another drill from the Remarkable Framework that can help you find those speaking opportunities.

But before you continue, turn to Chapter 10 on page 179. I created a worksheet there for you to write down your key takeaways from each chapter. This will reinforce what you're learning and help guide you through the Framework. You can also find a copy of this Key Takeaways worksheet in the workbook at remarkableframework.com.

CHAPTER 2
EMPOWER

Calm Before the Storm

True or false? If I learn how to be calm, I will be a great speaker. It's just my nerves that get in the way.

The answer is false. Imagine an ocean in the early morning. Its surface, smooth and flat, looks mysteriously calm. But there's turbulence and all kinds of animal life beneath the surface. You may not see that turbulence on the smooth surface, but it's there; a storm is brewing underneath.

As a keynote speaker, there are times when I still get nervous speaking. I may have a calm exterior when I'm presenting, but I am the first to admit that there are plenty of times when my nerves are sending chemical shockwaves through my system.

Nervousness may never go away. Never. So how can you cope with knowing that your nervousness may never go away? Do what I do … I breathe and reframe my thoughts.

"Fear is excitement without the breath," said Fritz Perls, psychotherapist and founder of Gestalt therapy. In his work, he discovered that the same systems in the body that produce fear also produce excitement. If you want to be calm, take a breath and reframe your fear as excitement. Feel the energy when you speak the words "I'm nervous" out loud. Then say "I'm excited." The same energy is present with both phrases, but it feels better when you're excited. Just try saying the word "excited" without smiling; it's almost impossible for the corners of your mouth not to turn up!

> From shit to shift is one letter away
> from making something happen.
>
> —Shelley Goldstein

Shift the words, and your energy and mindset will shift along with them. You can manage the shift by controlling your sympathetic and parasympathetic nervous systems—the two divisions of your autonomic nervous system (which controls involuntary bodily processes). These systems help to regulate your brain, body, mood, muscles, breath, heart rate, blood flow, and energy.

What's actually happening in your body when you feel nervous is that the sympathetic nervous system perceives the situation as threatening and activates the fight-or-flight response, which, in turn, releases cortisol and adrenaline into your bloodstream. As a result, your blood pressure goes up, your heart beats faster, your breathing becomes rapid, and you get distracted. Nervousness is clearly bad for your health—and your speaking! This is how you crumble under pressure, forget what you have to say, and fuel doubt.

But when you feel excitement, your body counters fight-or-flight by activating the parasympathetic nervous system to release the feel-good hormone dopamine as well as serotonin. Think of this as the rest-and-digest state. Your blood pressure drops, your heartbeat and breathing slow down, and you have better focus.

Your breath connects the brain with the body and helps you feel relaxed so that the nervous energy does not overwhelm your system. Excitement is good for your health and good for your speaking! In this state, you beam with confidence, achieve clarity, and thrive.

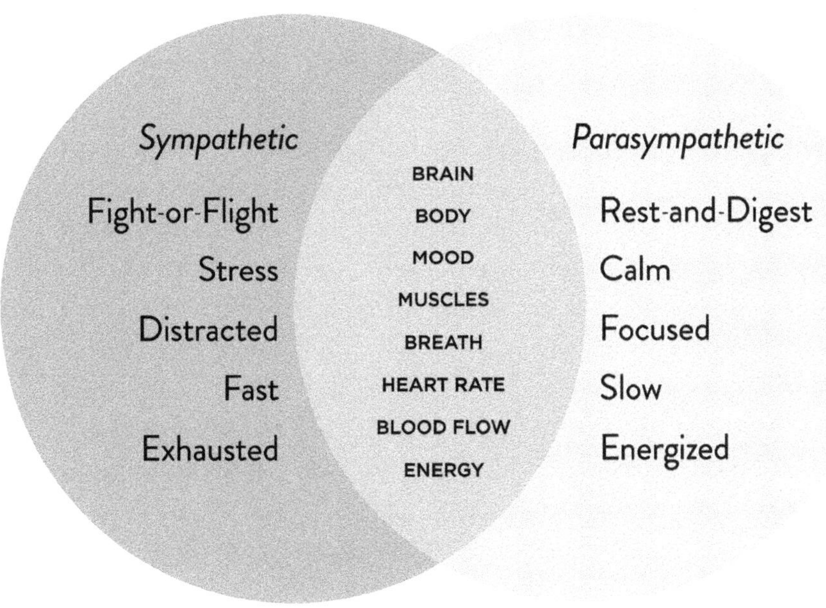

Your nervousness may never completely go away, but that can be a good thing. You want your adrenaline to get you motivated and ready (but with the reassurance that your dopamine will balance it out). With your breath to regulate you, you can show up in ways that don't leave you feeling completely paralyzed with fear and instead use that energy to empower your speaking.

As a high performer, you already have what it takes to reframe fear as excitement and embrace the unknown, which is where innovation materializes. As a business success, you understand that the unknown is good for business!

Of course, not every talk is exciting. There are difficult conversations that trigger nervousness and have nothing to do with excitement. You can't and shouldn't reframe these as something "exciting," so what can you do? In these situations, you can reframe fear as liberation. Sharing something difficult often brings a sense of relief, and that can feel liberating. The conversation can lead to a moment of growth with deeper connection and a new perspective.

A terrific drill to maintain the rest-and-digest state in your body when you start to feel overwhelmed is a simple technique called box breathing. It is often used by the United States Navy Seals and professional and amateur athletes, and is recommended by medical practitioners to reduce stress, restore calm, and get the excitable adrenaline and grounding dopamine pumping.

When box breathing, it's important to inhale as deeply as you exhale. You will feel a difference in just four cycles, but don't just think about breathing. I want you to feel cyclones of air moving around in your body. Maybe your shoulders rise with a big nourishing inhale. Maybe you feel a sigh of relief as your chest collapses on the exhale. I want you to breathe as if you're filling every cell in your body with oxygen.

You might even feel a little relaxed just reading this. So it's time to get more relaxed and box breathe. Follow these instructions or use my guided video on box breathing available in the Remarkable Framework playlist at my YouTube channel, youtube.com/@remarkablespeaking, or at remarkableframework.com in tandem with the Box Breathe section of the workbook.

Sit comfortably in a chair or a crossed-legged position on the floor.

Whatever phone calls, to-do lists, and emails are filling your inbox, put them all in a jar. Now put the jar on the other side of the door. I promise you, it'll be there when you're done with this drill.

Visualize a box like the following diagram. Follow the arrows around the four sides of the box, inhaling, holding, and exhaling for four counts on each side. Repeat this cycle four times.

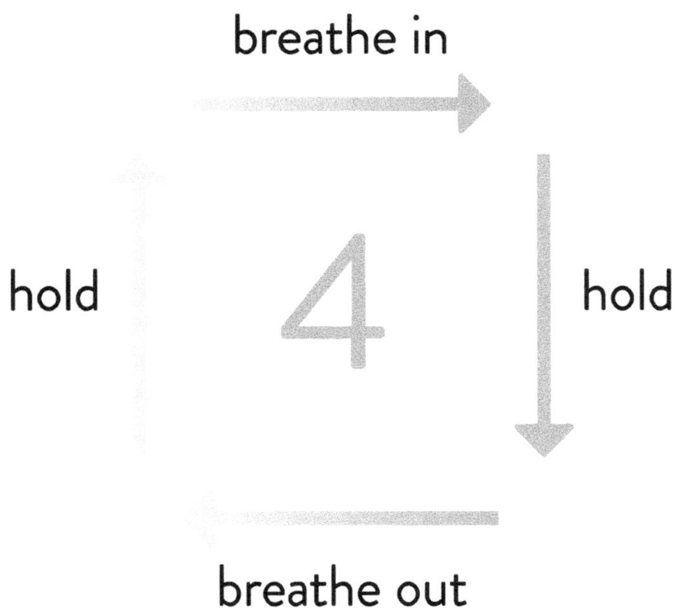

1. Breathe in for four long and steady counts.
2. Hold the breath in for four steady counts.
3. Breathe out for four long and steady counts.
4. Hold the breath out for four counts, long and steady.

> **PRO TIP:** As you breathe, visualize the movement of ocean waves. With each inhale, fill your body like the incoming tide of waves crashing onto the shore. With each exhale, release your breath like the outgoing tide as it recedes into the ocean. The holding of the breath is like the moment of suspension when the wave changes direction.

When you've completed the box breathing experience, consider how you feel. Has there been a shift in your body? Do you feel more relaxed?

These are the powerful effects of box breathing. As you read this book, you will discover just how convenient and beneficial the breath is in every aspect of your speaking.

Now that you're feeling calm, let's shake things up a bit.

Do Something That Scares You

A New Year's Day hike is a tradition for me. If you're not the last one to leave the party, it's a great way to start a new year.

So there I was on the trail, January 1, 2020. It was a gorgeous day. I was hiking with friends, and as some of us do around this time of year, we chatted our way through the hike making resolutions. We came along a bend in the trail, and I saw someone I recognized walking toward me. I was wracking my brain; where did I know him from? Then I realized it was Simon Sinek, renowned leadership author and public speaker who has one of the top twenty-five most-watched TED Talks of all time.

I've been listening to Simon for years. I've seen him talk in person. I've read his books. This was *the* author of *Start with Why*[8] walking toward me on New Year's Day. What a great way to start the year!

At first I was intimidated. This was my intellectual crush—and he's cute too! I had to say something clever, but my nerves hijacked my brain. So what came out of my mouth as we passed each other on the trail? "I love you." That's right, out of the blue I shrilled, "I love you!"

He probably thought I was a crazed fan. (Maybe I am.) But Simon didn't flinch; he said nothing and kept walking. I had the chance to give someone that I really admire a compliment, and of all the things that I could have said, I nervously blurted out the most nonsensical comment.

A few steps down the path, I decided to yell out, "Hey Simon, Happy New Year!" He responded with, "Happy New Year to you too!" Finally! I said something really absurd but followed up with something nice, and I was pleasantly surprised when he interacted. In that moment, I chose to do something scary, and it paid off. That was one of the few happier moments of 2020.

You want to feel confident? Do something that scares you.

As many TED Talks as there are out there, there are more people scared to death to get on that stage. This was the case for "Vanessa," a seasoned speaker I coached for her TEDx Talk. Here's how she described her experience:

> *I was seventh in line of nine speakers and I was the only standing ovation! Shelley talks about storytelling. She talks about vulnerability on stage and one of my biggest hold ups with learning the script was how to show up authentically.*
>
> *I always view TEDx Talks as being more of a professional place, not a place for emotion, not a place for tears and Shelley disagreed with me. My talk was a very sensitive topic and she gave me permission to show up vulnerable during my speech. But when you're going through it and rehearsing, you can't always let go of all preconceived*

> *notions of how it's supposed to be. She said to just go with my gut and I did. I got emotional on stage. It was incredibly impactful and beautifully authentic. I gave Shelley huge props for giving me permission to do that and for all the training in storytelling, in being authentic, in getting emotional, and she holds space for that.*

You may not be ready to do something as scary as a TED Talk just yet, but spoken interactions nonetheless will get your adrenaline and dopamine to flow, and they actually feel pretty good when all is said and done. Studies have found that confidence improves when you interact at work or in social situations.[9]

So find everyday opportunities to interact. Turn to the Speaking Opportunities worksheet (a sample of which I've included here) in the Speaking Opportunities section of your workbook.

SPEAKING OPPORTUNITIES WORKSHEET	
Opportunity 1	
Opportunity 2	
Opportunity 3	

For this next drill, set a timer for one minute and, on the worksheet, list three opportunities that you will have to speak or converse in the next twenty-four hours. I mean right after you finish this subchapter and put down this book, think of what calls or meetings you have on your schedule where you can initiate a conversation. Those are opportunities to interact, as is a networking event or collaboration with a colleague. It could be in-person or online—either counts as a speaking opportunity.

Your interaction can be non-work related, like going to a cafe and greeting the barista. Maybe you use the opportunity at the checkout at the market to ask the person next to you about an item in their cart. Or ask, "How are things looking around town today?" to a Lyft or bus driver.

Raise your hand during a webinar or presentation, even if you have nothing to say. Especially if you have nothing to say. A simple "Thank you" or "I appreciate your talk today" will get you there.

Comment on a social media post or type something into the chat during a workshop. Yes, commenting on social media or using chats are other pathways to practice confidence. Any one of these scenarios is your immediate opportunity to speak about something that feels a little scary. You don't have to be clever, you just have to say something.

Perhaps you think you don't have anything happening that's very exciting in the next twenty-fours hours. No big presentation or podcast? Reframe that thought! You have Zoom calls, meetings, team reviews, and more. You're doing something everyday, so I'm asking you to speak up *with the intention of interacting in these places* even if you haven't done so before.

If thoughts like "What will they think?" or "How will they respond?" come up, first practice a few tongue twisters to get out of your head.

If you feel scared, box breathe your way to feeling calm.

The key is to not let fear paralyze you. You may be surprised to know that acclaimed opera singer Luciano Pavarotti was so nervous when he walked on stage that he convinced himself, "I go to die."

Singing to sold-out opera houses all over the world, Pavarotti had no choice but to face his discomfort. He created a routine of breathing drills and reframed his self-talk to get himself on stage. The breath activated Pavarotti's parasympathetic nervous system, and by reframing his self-talk, he reduced his anxiety so that he could get on stage and deliver his famous and magnificent performances.

Pavarotti learned from his breath routine that if "You don't breathe, you don't sing."

The same applies to speaking. If you don't breathe, you don't speak.

As a high performer, you like challenges and pushing the limits. Trying to do hard things and going after what's never been done before is how you became successful. The pressure triggers your sympathetic nervous system, and you feel a rush of adrenaline. When you meet the challenge, you feel euphoric. "Wow, I did it!" And then you do it all over again because you realize that the rush of happiness was worth the risk of fear.

> The biggest voice is in my head,
> if it doesn't scare me, I'm not on the limit.
>
> —André Höflich, Winter Olympic snowboarder

PRO TIP: If you feel like you're at the edge of your comfort zone, keep pushing your limit.

PRO TIP: If something feels uncomfortable, do it again, and it will become more familiar.

PRO TIP: If what you're doing feels scary, breathe to relax.

In hindsight, whatever scary thing you do is never actually as scary as you think it is.

Okay, now that you've got a few opportunities and pro tips in your routine, gear up and put them into action to empower your speaking.

Take Ownership of the Throne

I used to work for a company where I was part of a senior leadership team. In many of the interdepartmental meetings, I was the sole female member. And I held the belief that I had to fight for my role in the company.

The CEO hired a consultant to advise us through our annual SWOT analysis, a process where the group identifies the company's strengths, weaknesses, opportunities, and threats to create a strategy for the future. As each member of the team contributed their ideas, I realized that it wasn't the men in the room that were challenging me, it was my negative self-talk telling me to fight because I didn't feel confident or respected.

Yet I hesitated to speak. It was that two percent of uncertainty looming in my head, thinking that my ideas were not that good. When one of the men presented a similar idea, the group cheered him on, "Great idea!" If my idea of good was "great" to others, then that was my cue to speak up—one hundred percent.

I raised my hand and presented my idea. I nervously rushed through the details, but the consultant and some of the men in that room cheered me on. "Great idea, Shelley, let's do it!" The satisfaction of hearing those words was confirmation that it was worth the risk. I knew my stuff, I owned my ideas. If I was there to serve the team, why wouldn't I share? It wasn't about who was sitting in the room; it was about what I brought to the room. At that moment, I was empowered, and my chair at the table felt more like I was sitting on a throne.

A chair's function is to keep you level with the table and prevent you from falling on the floor. A throne suggests a different function. Perhaps you sit up a little taller. Perhaps you're owning more of your life's experiences. When you take ownership of your ideas and experiences, it will give you the confidence to speak about them.

You know that feeling when you're really invested in something? Like your passion project, a biodiverse vineyard where you produce wine, or when you've just launched your nonprofit to build entrepreneurial communities in developing countries? That's ownership, a supercharger for confidence.

It empowers your speaking. I don't care how many speaking courses you sign up for or how many presentations you give, the day you take ownership of what you know, what you've experienced, and what you believe in is the day you present with remarkable confidence.

Remember King George VI? Though initially reluctant to take the throne, he practiced those silly tongue twisters to deliver one of the most memorable speeches of his reign: On September 3, 1939, he announced the United Kingdom's involvement in World War II. Taking ownership of his ideas motivated the king and those around him, and he won the respect of world leaders, his ministers, and the people of his country.

When you take ownership, you lead with ownership and inspire ownership in others. You empower them to take ownership of their ideas and their roles at every level. You're leading soldiers to become an army of corporals and generals.

> As we look ahead into the next century,
> leaders will be those who empower others.
>
> —Bill Gates

Ownership is about being clear on where you stand on an issue and speaking up in any situation. This gives you executive presence that replaces second guessing. It demonstrates initiative and increases the motivation and loyalty of the people you do business with and the people in your organization. Own your ideas and thoughts even if it feels scary to talk about them because if you don't, you're doing a disservice to yourself and the people that you serve.

Ownership also involves owning your mistakes or making decisions that are not popular. There's no more honest way to build trust with people than to admit you messed up and take accountability for how it impacts others, as long as you say it with confidence.

So reframe your selfish self-talk, allow yourself to step fully into your role, whatever it may be, and own your ideas and experiences. Breathe so your nerves are not controlling your body. You now know that they may never fully go away, and you can bet that you will never be one hundred percent ready. But you're reading this book, and that is as ready as you need to be.

Take a seat and take a moment to ask yourself, "Am I sitting on a chair or a throne?"

Make It a Great Experience

"What goes through the customer's mind? It's the place where they've had a great experience. You long forget about the price, but you never forget whether you had a good experience or a poor experience." Warren Buffet should know; he was successfully buying companies that prioritized great customer experiences as the cornerstone of their businesses.

When you're presenting or facilitating a meeting, how you deliver the information is what makes an impact. Think about the speakers that you've heard and had a great experience with. Maybe it was the keynote at a conference or a TED Talk. What was it that they said that moved you? Did they tell a story that reminded you of something in your life? Was it a situation they talked about that you could relate to? Think about those moments you felt connected. Did you nod in agreement? You were interacting with the speaker, and that made it a great experience.

If you dread meetings, like most people do, consider what it is about the experience that you don't like. Meetings, when they're effective, are important for doing business. So what would your ideal meeting need to be in order to make it a great experience? Stay tuned for more on that; I take a deeper dive into facilitating meetings in Chapter 9.

As a speaker, you're the meeting host, and that's your opportunity to set the tone and create the experience you want. People show up for meetings and don't really know what to expect. You can ask a few questions before things kick off like, "How's that project coming along?" Or, if it's the first time you're meeting people, introduce yourself and ask, "What brought you here today?"

PRO TIP: Start the conversation with a few icebreakers.

I was once giving a keynote about the unfair advantage of AI. Before we got started, I asked the hosts if anyone had recommendations for virtual assistants. The conversation started to flow, and I got a few referrals. By the time the event started, there was a familiar feeling buzzing through the room, like we were longtime friends.

Icebreakers and opportunities to connect on common ground are incremental ways to improve your speaking comfort. Interact and learn something about as many people as you can. Try out a few of the following icebreakers at your next meeting.

- You just read an article about the latest industry news. Ask someone how it relates to their business.
- Tell them you're reading a book to improve your speaking skills. Ask whether they're attending any professional development workshops.
- Ask if they can recommend any apps to improve daily productivity.

Maybe you work for an international organization or you're attending a tradeshow. People in a similar industry tend to talk a lot about the business. Mix up the conversation with some icebreakers about current events. You can find more in the Icebreakers section of the workbook at remarkableframework.com.

- Talk about the winning team from a sporting event or the latest series you binged.
- Maybe you just got back from a safari in South Africa. Ask if anyone has traveled there.
- Share a story about your pet and ask if they have pets. When I brought up the topic of pets as an icebreaker before a workshop I was leading, we discovered that two of the attendees owned tortoises!

One of the times when I was a guest on a podcast, the topic was producing both online and offline events. A few minutes before the host hit record, I mentioned that one of my favorite events was a specialty food show on the west coast. I had trained a team of cheesemakers on presentation skills. The host said he had just attended a fancy food show on the east coast. The conversation had us laughing about the added perks of sampling all of the gourmet treats. It set the mood for a recording full of friendly and lively conversation.

Prepare to be surprised, not by your nerves, but instead by discovering what you have in common with others. With icebreakers, you have more opportunities to interact and make speaking a great experience.

Power Up and Speak Up

A good maestro warms up the orchestra with scales before a performance. During rehearsals, conductor Leonard Bernstein pushed the musicians to reach for musical freedom. "It's got to be like one person singing his heart out and you're playing like an exercise," he said.

A good sports coach has the team run drills and stretch before game time on the court or field. Olympic gold-medal wrestler and coach Dan Gable explained it this way: "Gold medals aren't really made of gold. They're made of sweat, determination, and a hard-to-find alloy called guts."

A good yoga instructor leads the class through a series of sun salutations before they instruct the eight-angle pose. The whole yoga practice is designed sequentially to build warmth and flexibility in the body so you can move safely from the basic poses to the more advanced poses.

What maestros, coaches, and instructors all know is that practice creates a routine to form new habits, more opportunities to deliver a great experience, and the freedom to reach your highest potential.

The drills in this book are designed to help you power up and prime yourself to speak up. You can do them to warm up before an important call, presentation, or meeting and avoid a shaky start to your opening remarks. If you want to speak with confidence, make practice a requirement. If you want to improve your public speaking, you need to talk publicly.

You already speak every day—on the phone, on Zoom calls, at meetings, with customer service representatives. You interact with friends and family, conversing about all kinds of things. Look at each and every conversation as your opportunity to practice speaking every single day. And then practice reframing formal speaking events as engaging conversations.

> You don't have to be great to start,
> but you have to start to be great.
>
> —Zig Ziglar

The following Power Up drill will help you build a routine of speaking up. I do this drill routinely. My clients do this drill routinely. It's your time to start your routine.

Just go to remarkableframework.com or scan the QR code on the book cover and look for the Power Up section of the workbook.

Here's how the drill works in four steps:

STEP 1) Tongue Twisters and Say What?!: Do one each to get out of your head.

STEP 2) Reframe your chair into a throne, and take ownership of your ideas.

STEP 3) Find opportunities to interact and get comfortable. Make a list of potential speaking exchanges in the next twenty-four hours, and start conversations with icebreakers.

STEP 4) Box breathe for four cycles to restore calm.

Go to Chapter 10 on page 179 and write down your key takeaways for empowering your speaking. When you're finished, power up because in Chapter 3, you'll see how energy can add meaning to your words.

CHAPTER 3
MIC-DROP MOMENT

Channel Your Energy Into Expression

You're powered up with desire and determination. You can feel the energy.

If you yell at the top of your lungs, "**I FEEL EMPOWERED**," do you feel excited?

If you whisper under your breath, "I feel empowered," do you feel less excited?

That blast of energy, or lack of energy, reveals so much about how a speaker expresses themselves.

When preparing for a presentation, has anyone ever suggested that you should speak louder at a certain part to emphasize your point? Or told you to speak a little softer at the end of the third sentence because it would sound better if you had more musicality in your voice? Louder?

Softer? Musicality while speaking? Even if you have musical skills, you may wonder what they are talking about!

You don't need to be musical to be a good speaker, you just have to feel the energy in your body and express it to the outside world. According to neuroscientist and neurologist António R. Damásio, "We're not thinking machines that feel, we are feeling machines that think."

What Damásio suggests is that your emotions and feelings serve as a pathway to how you think and learn. The flow of energy through the body that you feel exists because emotions start as sensations in the body. When you have a physical feeling about something, you develop emotions that you can identify through thought, such as excitement or happiness, anger or rage.

In his book *Emotional: The New Thinking About Feelings*,[10] author Leonard Mlodinow explains that emotions are interconnected to how you think and behave. Emotions are your tools for survival. They help you navigate and adapt to different circumstances. Emotions are crucial to your decision-making processes and empower you to go after your goals.

Take the Wright brothers for example. The Wright brothers didn't just wake up one day in December 1903 and launch the Flyer into aviation history at Kitty Hawk, North Carolina. Decades of effort from dozens of inventors who faced countless setbacks and failures led to that moment.

Taking into account all of the industrious aviators of that time, it was the Wright brothers who persevered. Motivated by emotions of curiosity and determination, they refined their invention to claim success where others had given up.

Contrary to popular belief, being emotional is not a bad thing.

Emotional. Winston Churchill, Margaret Thatcher, John F. Kennedy, Oprah Winfrey, Martin Luther King Jr., and Malala Yousafzai—some of the world's most compelling speakers—all express emotion. As a speaker, you're sharing your opinions and ideas because they have meaning to you. When something has meaning, you express it with emotion.

Have you watched TED Talks? Many of them are about people who share their journey to overcoming an obstacle. Some speakers have experienced a devastating failure and won against all odds. They share their life-altering moments and the lessons learned getting to the other side. Their journeys *are filled with emotion.*

Read the following descriptions for three of the top twenty-five most-watched TED Talks[11] of all time. What is it about each one that you connect to? You can find hyperlinks to these full talks in the Videos: How-To and More section of the workbook.

"My Stroke of Insight," by Dr. Jill Bolte Taylor. Dr. Taylor, a neuroscientist, had the unique opportunity to study the impacts of her own stroke as she was having it in real time. In her talk, she chronicles how she found nirvana as an option over fear and anxiety.

In "My Philosophy for a Happy Life," seventeen-year-old Sam Berns tells how he refused to let a very rare genetic disorder hold him back from living a happy life. He describes his struggles, and, as a young person, reminds listeners that "Being brave isn't supposed to be easy."

In "The Power of Vulnerability," Dr. Brené Brown, a research professor, shares her study on human disconnection due to feelings of shame and worthiness. She found out the hard way, realizing it was her struggle too. She admits, "It was a yearlong street fight. It was a slugfest. Vulnerability pushed, I pushed back. I lost the fight, but probably won my life back."

Few successful people start out great. It's their emotional journey that makes you feel connected with them. You may feel less compassionate about Sarah Blakely when you hear she is a billionaire. However, when you learn about the challenges she faced when she started Spanx while selling fax machines door-to-door, you might empathize because her story is somewhat similar to yours. Emotions make us all human.

> For there is always light,
> if only we're brave enough to see it,
> if only we're brave enough to be it.
>
> —Amanda Gorman

If you're moved by others' journeys of failures, successes, heartache, and happiness, perhaps you're starting to feel a little emotional about your own personal journey.

When you're focused on outcome instead of what you're experiencing in real time, you'll miss those mic-drop moments that help you express your story. Sharing how you feel about what you're saying fosters a sense of connection with others, creating a safe space for them to do the same. This self-awareness nurtures empathy and understanding, the building blocks of strong relationships. Recognizing your emotions, you start to realize you're not traveling on the journey alone.

Tapping into your emotions or being emotional does not mean you're out of control. There are degrees of emotions and many words for you to use to describe how you feel.

Research about the origins of emotion and how it works in the body is ongoing.[12] But to help you understand the range of emotion in the context of speaking, I've created the Feeling Finder, a spin on the Plutchik Wheel.[13]

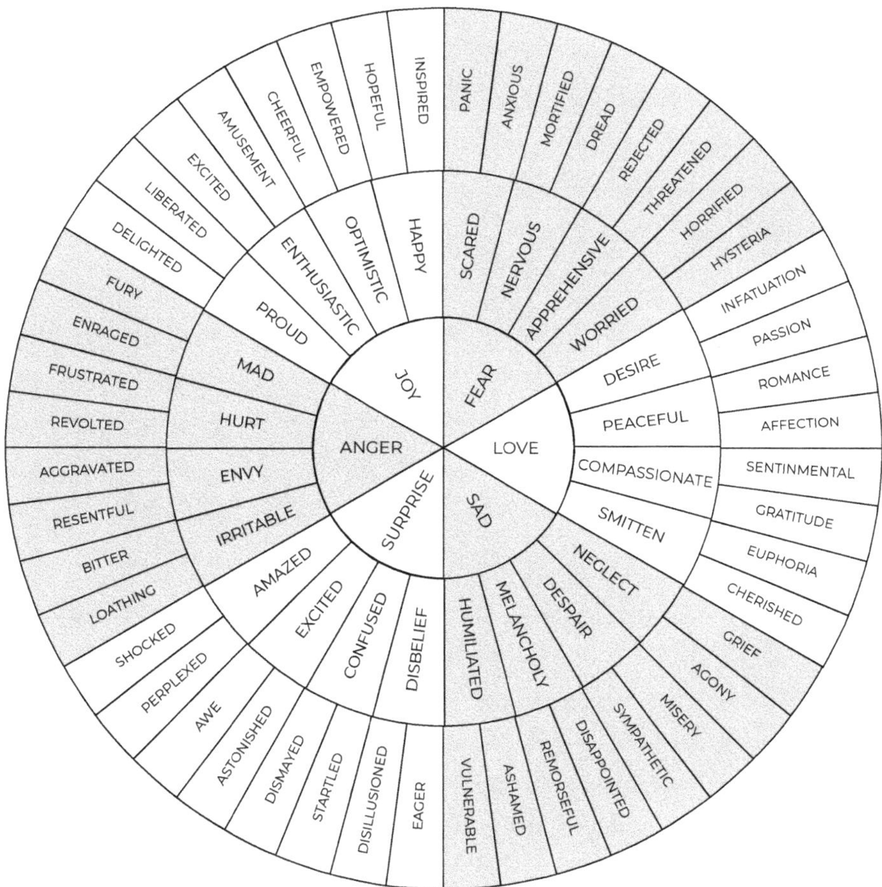

Imagine two people walking into a room filled with puppies. Their first reaction is feeling surprised. Start with the word surprise in the center of the Feeling Finder. It's one of six basic emotions.

Look to the middle tier of the Finder to see how the word can be expressed with more nuance or intensity, such as amazed, excited, or disbelief. Both people have the same experience of surprise when they see the puppies, but each person may have a different way of feeling surprised. One person might feel amazed and the other in disbelief.

Surprise gets more specific in the outermost tier with words like shocked, perplexed, eager, and so on. The person that is in disbelief may actually be feeling more specifically in awe of the puppies.

So while two people may witness the same room filled with puppies, their experiences of it, and the resulting emotions, can vary drastically due to their unique sensibilities: their mood, their body's sensations, and their surroundings. Researchers found that the mind creates mental maps based on how people feel and what they've experienced.[14] These sensibilities shape how they perceive, interpret, and respond to the world around them, which gives everyone different perspectives.

Emotion is considered the language of feelings, so once you identify words on the Feeling Finder that express how you feel, you can embody the feeling, making it easier to talk about your experiences. Feelings last longer, which helps you recall memories. Choosing words to identify your feelings allows you to manage your reaction, like de-escalating a situation, and communicate your message with less ambiguity.

Gestures also communicate emotion. Have you ever considered what your gestures are saying when you're speaking? In the book *The Extended Mind*, Annie Murphy Paul writes, "Gestures don't merely echo or amplify spoken language; they carry out cognitive and communicative functions that language can't touch. Where language is discrete and linear—one word following another—gesture is impressionistic and holistic, conveying an immediate sense of how things look and feel and move."[15] In other words (pun intended), gestures serve as a nonverbal form of communication that can complement or even replace spoken language.

I have clients that push back on incorporating expression and emotion—whether by words or gestures—into their speaking. "I would never communicate with emotion in that way!" Then I bring up that time they mentioned people thought they sounded like a robot when they spoke. I've come to understand that if you want to amaze audiences, you need to let them know how amazed you are. The energy in your body is the fuel that brings your amazing story to life.

> Lose your mind and come to your senses!
>
> —Fritz Perls

So the next time somebody suggests that you should add musicality to your speech, tap into your energy and ask, "How do I *feel* about what I'm saying?"

When You Care, They Care

While the bottom line is that your products or services make money, they also might be designed to help people improve their lives or even save lives. How significant is that to you? Probably very significant.

As a client and consumer, would you make a purchase from a company or person you don't know or trust? Probably not.

You want to feel good about doing business as a supplier or a customer, so, naturally, your caring goes beyond the immediate transaction. Likewise, when you're speaking, you want people to understand the significance of what you're saying and why you're saying it beyond a quick pitch. When you reflect on your experiences to illustrate why you care, you may feel a strong emotion and want to hold back from expressing it. But here's the thing, you cannot simply talk yourself out of the emotion and expect your words to convey any meaning.

I remember hearing Simon Sinek explain how Phil Knight, the former CEO of Nike and a runner himself, reflected on a mic-drop moment from a runner's journey:

> *He was speaking at a large conference and he said to the audience, 'If any of you have ever run for exercise, can you please stand up?' Most of the room stood up. He said, 'If you run at least once a week, please keep standing.' Most of them sat. He says, 'If you run three times a week, rain or shine, regardless of the weather or the temperature, please keep standing.' There's now a smattering of people and he says, 'The next time you're out there, before the sun is up, it's dark, it's cold, and it's wet, and you're running by yourself. We're the ones standing under the lamppost cheering you on.' That's how he described Nike, and in an instant, you understand what 'Just Do It' means. It has nothing to do with winning. It has everything to do with doing.*

You can't discount the vividness and emotional impact of that mic-drop moment. If you're that runner, you feel motivated and valued as part of a bigger movement. That lamppost not only illustrates the significance of Nike's brand, it explains the meaning of why people buy its running shoes. Because on those days when you're struggling to get started or ready to give up, you know Nike cares about you.

You too care about your clients, partners, and colleagues, both current and future. And when you tap into and share with them all the time, sweat, and tears you put into your journey to build that company or launch that product, you convey that care and dedication. Those memories and emotions have everything to do with your purpose. Maybe you reminisce about the first day you started a new job—did you feel anxiety onboarding or were you eager to face the challenges? How did you feel during your first meeting, your first deal, and your first failure? These examples are situations that are driven by emotions. Using the Feeling Finder, you get to decide what words match the way you feel to best identify your emotions. Thus, you can more accurately express yourself and convey empathy, and that's when people will *know* how much you care.

No Knowing the
destination without
first starting
the journey

How else would angel investors know whether you're the right executive they should invest in? How else would prospects know if you have their best interests in mind? How else would employees know if you're a trusted leader?

> I raise up my voice—not so that I can shout,
> but so that those without a voice can be heard.
>
> —Malala Yousafzai

Cofounder and executive chairman of LinkedIn Reid Hoffman coauthored the book *The Alliance*.[16] The book focuses on the idea that the employer-employee relationship is broken because few invest in long-term relationships. He suggests organizations invest in salaries and onboarding new hires while acknowledging that many employees do not feel that they can speak honestly about their work or feel underappreciated because their direct reports are unaware of their full capabilities. Hoffman's realization?

There's a lack of trust in most organizations because you don't think they care and they don't think you care.

Whether it's Phil Knight talking about Nike or me sharing my personal journey, sharing mic-drop moments reveals your purpose as a visionary and connects your brand with a human story.

> People don't care how much you know,
> until they know how much you care.
>
> —Theodore Roosevelt

Whether challenging, exhilarating, or barely surviving, you can paint a picture of your journey with your mic-drop moments. Expressing your emotions will pull your audience in, curious to hear what happens next. Following along, they feel empathy and compassion. It's how you establish trust and what gets you excited to share your big ideas with the world. Caring starts with you.

When it comes to sharing, how much is too much? Continue reading and see how things start to click.

Sharing and Oversharing

When people realize they have things in common, they often say, "We really clicked!" It turns out that the "click" is a neural coupling in the brain that happens when the listener's brain is mirroring the speaker's.[17]

Neuroscience professor Uri Hasson says the effects of storytelling are essential in communicating because, "You're going to understand me better, you're going to have similar feelings to the feeling that I am having, and you're going to remember it better."[18]

I have a client, "Henry," that has been in tech sales for several years. Henry came to me with a well-rehearsed pitch summarizing every feature and benefit from the sales one-sheet. When I asked him questions about the product, he would rinse and repeat more of the same.

We trained and turned his eight-minute run-on sentence into an engaging conversation. I had Henry share personal experiences about his home renovation as a metaphor to explain the value of the product he was selling. There was barely a mention of features and benefits in what became an un-pitch of less than three minutes. Everyone in the room, his team included, was captivated by how he presented the product and the prospect signed the purchase order.

Two things happened in the following days. First, the prospect, turned customer, called Henry offering him a job because they were so impressed with his delivery. Second, Henry's impressive delivery had such a strong impact that senior management promoted him to public speaking mentor for the entire sales team.

As an entrepreneur, you might have to pitch investors, rally your team, or even explain a new strategy to clients. Talking about a relatable experience, personal or professional, to describe the transformation of a product or situation is how people will understand you, connect with you, and remember your solution.

People give product overviews and ambiguous project summaries all day long. But if you shared one pivotal, significant moment for that product or project, you could spark real interest. That moment may be all you need to share before your audience says, "Really? Tell me more!"

Stories are memorable because of how someone feels at the moment they hear what you say. Martin Luther King Jr.'s "I Have a Dream" speech, considered one of the most iconic speeches of all time, moved millions and still has that impact on people to this day. Dr. King wrote several drafts of the speech originally titled "Normalcy, Never Again" with no mention of a dream.[19] The crowds were stirring as he spoke at the Lincoln Memorial in Washington, D.C., on August 28, 1963. It was Dr. King's friend, gospel singer Mahalia Jackson, who had heard him speak on this topic many times before and interjected, "Tell 'em about the dream, Martin, tell 'em about the dream!" In that moment of passion, Dr. King embodied his dream and the words transcended his script. That moment clicked, and history was made.

That was my experience with every story and quote I included in this book. I was moved in some way when I first experienced each one. Something clicked. Perhaps something I've said has clicked with you too.

There are many stories and experiences you can share about your journey in business and your personal life. But when is a story too personal or too private to share?

Personal could be a moment when you spilled your coffee on the quarterly report or you had a discussion about a client that is always past due on their invoices. Both are relatable personal experiences.

Private could be a moment that is more profound or troubling, like a close colleague dealing with a serious illness or a discussion about a client that is always past due on their invoices.

See what I did there?

When telling a story, there's a point where sharing becomes oversharing, especially in professional situations. The reasons for oversharing may come from nerves and adrenaline spikes because you feel socially anxious, wanting to belong and connect with others. That nervousness can lead you to share too much, too fast.

If you choose to share something deeply private, it's important to make sure that you can speak about it with resoluteness and certainty. If not, it may not be a forum to spill your guts.

Take into account if what you're sharing will benefit your audience. If you know about their challenges first-hand, they will appreciate that you've had a similar experience.

When in doubt, respect confidentiality. Use your discretion to share only what is necessary information or choose to be silent, omitting the details all together.

> **PRO TIP:** Be curious to get perspective. Asking icebreaker questions allows you to gauge who's ready to share and hear sensitive moments.

> **PRO TIP:** Reframe the discussion and turn the focus to another topic. If you notice your audience is fidgeting uncomfortably or looking away with apprehension, that may be a signal that you're overwhelming them.

> **PRO TIP:** Take a breath before you speak and ask yourself, is every detail that you're sharing important for people to understand your point?

Your mic-drop moments, personal or private, are the way to connect with people and serve them in a way that you, as a leader, know will help them.

According to Prof. Hasson, "You can use storytelling as a way to transport people into your experiences and make them live your memories."[20]

Essentially, comprehension, connection, and being memorable are the trifecta of great speaking where storytelling is, literally, a meeting of the minds.

And the Oscar Goes to ...

Speaking is not a performance. That includes presenting, leading a workshop, or selling. Leave performing to the professional actors who portray different characters and win an Oscar award for doing so.

Professional actors are technically trained to act with all the production elements in a theatrical setting. They have a script and rehearse every word and movement. This ensures that their performances go exactly as planned. But to be an authentic speaker, precision movements and technicalities can fail you. Because the minute you start feeling panic, your sympathetic nervous system goes into overdrive and your brain draws a blank.

When I was learning to play golf, my dad would take me out on the course at the end of the day. With nine holes-in-one and a single-digit handicap, his swing was natural and fluid. As I approached the tee, he would always remind me of one thing, "Visualize where you want the ball to land."

Later, I would take lessons from a golf pro who had a habit of calling out a constant stream of cues while I was swinging the club. "Keep your hands soft, but don't get handsy. Swing the club on the plane, but don't pull. Rotate and release your upper body, but don't sway." It takes about 1.5 seconds to swing a club. My brain couldn't digest half of what the pro said, let alone swing. I was completely frustrated, and there was nothing natural about the process.

It's not that different when you have a carefully planned speech. "Raise your volume on the last word in the first sentence, but lower your voice on the first word of the fifth paragraph. Make sure you highlight the metric on slide six, but keep your eyes on the audience and don't forget to smile!" Recalling all those technical cues in 1.5 seconds and it's no wonder you're nervous about presenting. And it's no wonder you might sound like a robot.

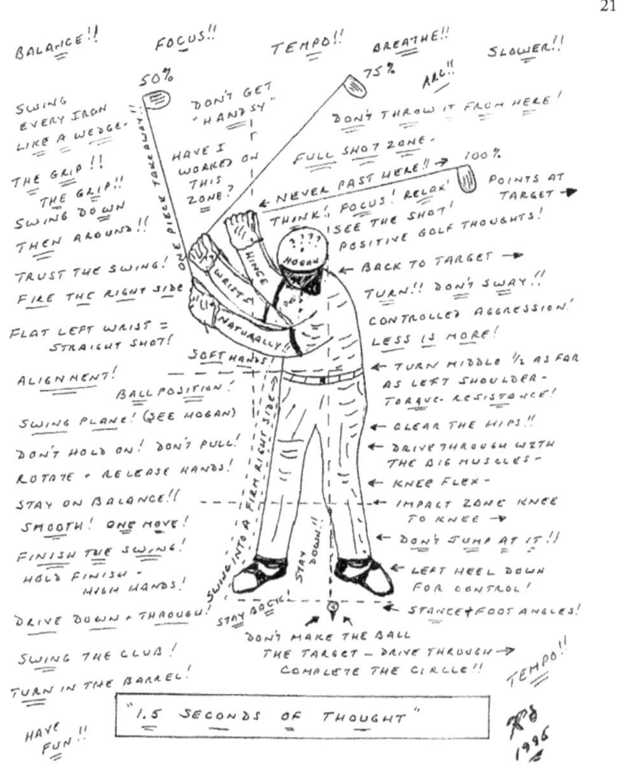

Speaking from the heart is how you present with genuine spontaneity because when you're talking about something that you've experienced, your authenticity emerges from the emotion that you feel. The audience will find you more relatable and connect better with your story when your speaking is conversational.

You can practice speaking from the heart by turning to the Feeling Finder section in the workbook at remarkableframework.com.

Pick one of the three opportunities you identified on Chapter 2's Speaking Opportunities worksheet. Next, using the Feeling Finder, find two emotions that match the way you felt about that experience.

- First, start in the center of the Feeling Finder and choose one of the six basic emotions.
- Second, look to the middle tier to explore your feelings with more nuance or intensity.
- Third, select from the emotions in the outermost tier to get even more specific.

Now set a timer for one minute and talk about your experience from the perspective of one of the emotions. Set a timer for another minute; repeat the story but from the perspective of the second emotion. Notice how in each perspective of the story you speak more spontaneously and authentically.

PRO TIP: Looking at the Feeling Finder, ask yourself this question: "How do I feel about that moment?"

PRO TIP: It's okay to experience more than one emotion. The more you can identify your emotions, the better you can manage them and improve your communication with others.

PRO TIP: A daily routine that includes the Power Up drill will free your thinking and help you access your words more naturally and authentically.

Practice retelling this story a few more times to get comfortable connecting fluidly with your emotions and speaking freely from different perspectives. But beware of over-rehearsing, which can actually increase anxiety. The more focused you are on perfecting your words, the more robotic and performative you'll appear.

Leave the performances for Broadway or the movies. Use the 1.5 seconds to breathe and rest your mind instead of overloading your head with technical cues. You're not trying to be pithy. You're not trying to *act* authentic. You're *being* your authentic self. Share what's important to you, and let your emotions do the talking.

Audiences connect to authentic speakers. That's what draws them into the conversation unlike an over-rehearsed melodrama. You might make a few mistakes, but there's no character development or script required.

On that note, in the next subchapter, I'll share how a few mistakes can enhance your human connection without sidetracking the conversation.

The Unexpected Applause: Your Blooper Reel

Do you ever stick around for the blooper reel after you watch a movie or show? You know, the outtakes where all the actors make mistakes and mess up their lines? There is usually some really funny stuff going on, and sometimes the bloopers are funnier than the show itself. There are actually shows built around bloopers and outtakes.

Bloopers can ruin a performance, but they also can bring authenticity to your presentations. Imagine you're giving a presentation and you make a mistake. Instead of falling apart, worried that your speech isn't perfect, embody the moment as a blooper. Everyone has made mistakes one time or another, and it is natural to flub lines or pull up the wrong slide for your presentation. When you make light of the situation and make it part of the conversation, you'll feel more at ease and your audience will, therefore, feel more at ease because everyone can relate. It's a moment of pure human connection.

I once saw an interview with comic Paul Reubens where he spoke about how he created the character of Pee-wee Herman. It came about because early in his career doing standup in comedy clubs, he was so nervous that he couldn't remember the punchlines to his jokes. He would get on stage and fail miserably. Unfortunately for him, it wasn't the jokes people were laughing at.

Reubens, however, embraced his mistakes and created a goofy character that was a bad comic—a character determined to get booed off the stage.

"I just told jokes where I couldn't remember the lines and pulled props out of the bag." Working with what he had in his prop bag, Reubens' Pee-wee stood out as a unique and memorable comedian. His success kept audiences laughing with him for decades.

Like Reubens, you won't get it right every time, and that's okay because making mistakes could be your next mic-drop moment—or punchline. If you want authenticity, work with what you have.

A global software company hired me to facilitate a workshop for 150 team members. Also in attendance were senior-level managers. When I was introduced, I thanked the group and the VP of program management and accidentally mispronounced her name. She corrected me, and I said, "My mistake, I'll be sure to get it right on your paycheck." Everyone laughed, including the VP. No harm, no foul, and I continued to lead the workshop. What could have been an incredibly awkward moment turned into a moment of connection. Everyone in the room—including the VP—could relate to mispronouncing a name!

> If I had to live my life again
> I'd make all the same mistakes, only sooner.
>
> —Tallulah Bankhead

Hiding your mistakes to fake your way through a perfect presentation will bring more attention to them. Perfection is for the editing room.

We all make mistakes. You'll have a laugh, and maybe your audience will laugh with you too.

Transcend Your Words

You may have thought a job at Ringling Bros. was the pinnacle of my career, but I leveraged my skills years later and launched a branding and marketing consultancy called Big Idea in 1999.

As a marketer, I found networking to be an opportunity to expand my business. And my circus stories were a great icebreaker. After a live event, I would shuffle through the pile of business cards I collected and struggle to remember each person who had given me one. As a result, half the pile went into the trash. That gave me the idea to design my business card as a visual description of what I do. Handing out my card became an icebreaker in and of itself.

About seven years later, I got a call from a senior advisor who worked for a utility company. He was looking to hire someone for a branding project and said, "You had that really cool business card. I will never forget when you handed it to me."

The impact of something as unique as design can also be applied when you share stories as a speaker. Telling a story, drawing a picture in the minds of your audience, instead of simply stating the facts, allows your words to transcend their literal meaning and have a bigger impact.

Watching legendary cellist Yo-Yo Ma play, you will see that he appears to enter a flow state, as if his body and the cello are one unit, embodying each note to create the music. "My practice is so that I can transcend it," explains Ma. "If I spend a hundred percent of my brain real estate concentrating on how I'm going to do something, I'm going to feel nothing. So if I can decrease the amount of brain real estate on the playing aspect of the cello, I can focus on what it's about. That is when music begins to speak."

When I speak from a flow state, or "in the zone" as athletes refer to this state, I'm so deeply engaged with my purpose that I lose sense of self-consciousness, and time feels suspended.

My clients have witnessed this first-hand. I had coached "Jomei" in a group training for advanced speaking skills. Six months later, he reached out again—this time for one-on-one training specifically on how to pitch service proposals as a recent retiree turned consultant. When we reconnected, he emphasized what a strong impression my coaching had on him in our previous sessions. I was grateful for his kind words and asked what specifically I had said that he connected with. He replied that it wasn't one particular thing that I'd said, but, rather, it was how I made him feel during our sessions. "You are the coach whisperer,"Jomei said about my coaching, "You got us to tap into our emotions and explore our feelings without asking us to do so." His testimonial reminded me to look back at what other clients have said.

"Shelley is so *passionate*, so present, in the moment, she inspires me!"

"Shelley has this very dynamic personality, which is just incredible, and the way she speaks is so *impassioned*."

"Shelley is so clear the way she models public speaking, clearly *passionate* and highly skilled!"

My clients' experiences of my coaching transcend beyond any one thing I say or do. By expressing the best version of myself, they can feel just how much I care for their success.

Maybe you've experienced something similar when you heard a keynote speech or podcast; you don't remember the exact words that person said, but you remember the moment that you were moved.

Now consider how your own words might have moved the people around you; maybe it's your courageous outlook or your ability to push boundaries and challenge the status quo that have impacted them. They feel your passion.

It's not necessarily each word that you say, it is how you embody the meaning of your message that leaves a lasting impression. Your sympathetic nervous system releases dopamine, and you're sitting on that throne feeling pretty good. That's when mic-drop moments transcend people beyond a design, beyond the notes, and beyond your words.

> Your self-expression allows the audience to have their own self-expression.
>
> —Rick Rubin

At this stage of your speaking journey, you've learned about reframing your negative thoughts, where to find opportunities to empower yourself, and why sharing your experiences is important if you want to be a remarkable speaker.

Before you take the next step to activation, jot down your key takeaways for mic-drop moments in Chapter 10 on page 180.

Additionally, you've got the Power Up drill, and, along with your routine, you trust yourself more. But if you don't speak up, you're not a public speaker. In Chapter 4, you'll learn how to elevate your speaking in public.

CHAPTER 4 ACTIVATE

If You're Uncomfortable, You're in the Right Place

Have you ever learned a new language? Not unlike the experience of learning to ride a bike that I talked about earlier, the uncertainty of pronouncing the words probably took you out of your comfort zone, and self-judgments likely crept in. But the more conversations you had with people, the more fluent you became, and the more comfortable you started to feel speaking it.

It's the same with public speaking. Because speaking in different situations is new and unfamiliar, it's going to feel a little uncomfortable, and it's going to take some time to master. It's okay, you're still in the right place.

I've studied different methods of public speaking, but regardless of the method, my speaking skills always improved because I made a point of applying the practice of speaking up in front of people to make the theory stick.

The practice … the hands-on method of "doing it" … that is what helps you start to feel comfortable and positions you to become an excellent speaker. Each time you show up to speak, reframe the situation as just another conversation. One of your most attainable practices is through networking opportunities. You can network at conferences and tradeshows, or through networking-specific events that happen every day. In addition to making connections and building relationships, networking is a low-risk opportunity to practice speaking.

> Always go a little further into the water than you feel you're capable of being in. Go a little bit out of your depth and when you don't feel that your feet are quite touching the bottom, you're just about in the right place to do something exciting.
>
> —David Bowie

Over the last few years, a lot of networking has moved online. The format is typically a series of breakout rooms with three or four people per room. Each person gets one minute to talk about what they do. One after the other, the majority of the attendees state their job title followed by a series of features and benefits about their business and maybe a crafty tagline.

I was attending an online networking event, and, in my one-minute introduction, I shared my experience with a client, "Penelope," who was having trouble landing job interviews as a zoologist. Her uncle said she had a learning disability. She told me she got nervous during interviews and didn't know the right thing to say. I explained I was not able to diagnose her, however, I let the family know I could help Penelope find her voice. After I coached her, she got not one but three job offers sharing her hilarious escapades caring for the flamingos.

I never mentioned my title, my company, or my services during my one minute. I let the story describe what I do, and, personally, it was a very meaningful experience for me. Attendees in the breakout room followed up with me, saying they were moved by what I said and wanting to know how they could get results like my client.

> I have to be seen to be believed.
>
> —Queen Elizabeth II

Queen Elizabeth II understood that being seen meant not just visibly showing up, but showing up in a meaningful way. From world leaders to factory workers, she took the time to listen to their point of view and embraced their differing beliefs. People felt seen and heard, and her compassionate approach enabled her to gain their trust. A study in leadership, the queen with a servant's heart embodied her sense of purpose, holding the throne for seventy years.

Sharing your mic-drop moments are what moves people because they get to see you for who you really are. Your honesty and transparency make people feel safe and perhaps a little more comfortable. Creating a safe space starts with you showing up and talking about your journey from your heart.

The next time you're in a networking event or conference, I want you to simply share a mic-drop moment. Avoid reciting the details on your business card or benefits on your website, and say something more meaningful. If you recall from Chapter 3, my business card had only an intriguing graphic, but it was more than enough to facilitate discussion.

There are lots of realtors, lawyers, and doctors out there in the world; what makes you different? Was there a client experience that you could share as an opening remark without saying you're a realtor? By sharing that story, you help people understand what *kind* of realtor you are beyond your title.

Attend networking groups, and when it's your turn to say what you do, don't do it! Instead, lead in with a story, and I guarantee that you'll stand out in the crowd. There will be plenty of time to talk about your contact details when people ask how they can follow up.

> **PRO TIP:** Avoid listing off your job title, company, and benefits. When it's your turn to speak, share a mic-drop moment. Talk about a pivotal moment in your career that changed something for you. That's it. One learning moment that inspired you to do what you do.

There are endless networking groups available online and offline for every industry. Some are referral-based, and most are free to attend. You can source groups through your local chamber of commerce or Rotary clubs. You can do a search on LinkedIn or associations for industry, trade, and alumni events. You will feel uncomfortable at first. But the more groups you attend, the more opportunities you will have for conversation, and the more familiar speaking will become.

I know that speaking up in those rooms can take a lot of energy. It can be exhausting, and this alone can hold you back, so it's important to have different ways to manage your energy. A few rounds of box breathing will help you not waste your energy on being nervous. Practicing some tongue twisters before attending will quell any judgments you may have.

When it's your turn to introduce yourself, share a moment from your journey. You'll get to practice speaking, make new connections, and you might even sign new clients. Now you're activating your potential.

No Surrender

No surrender. As a war reference, *no surrender* means perseverance and never giving up what you believe in.

"No Surrender" also is a Bruce Springsteen song that suggests life is not ideal: "You compromise, you suffer defeat, you slip into life's gray areas."

As a leader, *no surrender* means excelling at tackling challenges head-on. If you don't feel ready to speak because you're feeling nervous about the topic or perhaps the conference organizer changed the format at the last minute, persevere—one hundred percent readiness is not a requirement for success.

So how do you reconcile *no surrender* with receiving *no* as an answer?

The word *no* sounds and feels awful. The client that you're presenting to may reject your idea, and you may never learn why. The rejection can feel heavy, but what's important to remember is that it's not personal. Ask yourself as the tenacious leader you are, do you persevere for what you believe in or surrender at the first sign of *no*?

I am reminded of a quote from Byron Katie: "You can have anything you want in life if you're willing to receive 1,000 NOs." If you detach from the outcome in a situation and focus on what you have or can do, you'll feel greater satisfaction.

A definite *yes* outcome is out of your control and adds undue pressure to an already stressful situation. You can take ownership and reframe your self-talk to feel comfortable. Imagine what your day would look like if your goal was to collect one thousand *nos*?

When Howard Schultz joined Starbucks in 1982, investors said *no* because they were not convinced the market was ready to pay five dollars for a cup of coffee. Schultz persevered and transformed how people drink coffee and created a lifestyle that has been adopted around the globe.

Arlan Hamilton, founder and managing partner of Backstage Capital, heard *no* because less than two percent of women and minority leaders were represented in the venture capital world. While homeless herself, Hamilton attended pitch meetings and built a firm that has invested in over two hundred startups, believing in the future of women, BIPOC, and LGBTQIA+ entrepreneurs.

Before starting Disneyland, Walt Disney was fired by the *Kansas City Star* for not being creative enough. Editors said *no* to early versions of Mickey Mouse because people cringed at the sight of rodents. Refusing to compromise, the globalization of the mouse now generates over eighty-eight billion dollars worldwide.

Hedy Lamarr, a 1930s film icon and inventor, did not surrender when the Navy said *no* to her frequency-hopping technology. Instead, she patented her revolutionary invention in 1942; it ultimately became the precursor to Wi-Fi, GPS, and Bluetooth, earning her the title "mother of Wi-Fi."

There are times when your nerves are going to get the best of you because you really, really want your speech to land with people. And you're going to hear *no*. Refrain from saying to yourself: "I should've had a better story. I should've done the slide differently. I should've asked about that solution." A dear friend of mine has a great response to those nagging self-criticisms: "Stop *shoulding* all over yourself!" Reframe "I should" with "I get to do something."

You'll learn to let go of the outcome and get comfortable hearing *no*. Activated by a *no surrender* spirit, you'll feel motivated because speaking up is the real reward.

Speaking up starts with one conversation at a time. Let's chat more about that next.

Let's Chat

Interacting with your audience before you present your talk can override the fear of thinking that you don't have anything valuable to say. Knowing a little more about them will give you insight into why what you have to say has value.

And what if they are skeptical or disagree with your message? That's okay. It's healthy to disagree. It happens all the time during the workday when you're problem solving, negotiating salaries, and seeking conflict resolution. If someone disagrees, keep the discussion conversational. "Thank you, I see where you're coming from." Let them know that you're interested to hear what they think about your idea when you share your perspective.

One of the more interesting risks I ever took was when I was a guest on a podcast, and I challenged the hosts. One of the hosts, a millennial marketer, admitted she hated social media. I responded that I had reasons she would love it by the end of the episode. Of course she was skeptical: "If you can make me love social media, you're a genius!"

"Humans like to interact," I said, "so what if you approached social media as a conversation, a way to interact, instead of as a platform for blasting posts?" You see, I wanted to encourage them to have more conversations. Like a podcast, social media also is an opportunity for conversation.

The hosts then took a question from the audience about what to do when feeling anxiety about creating content. My advice was that the first step is to have a conversation. When I create content, I'm not making it to be clever; I'm having a conversation with people I want to help. That takes the pressure off because, not unlike conversations you have with friends over a casual dinner, there's not much at stake.

I also pointed out that there's no elaborate social media strategy. Just start a dialogue. Conversations are a natural way to build relationships, and relationships are how people do business. That idea lowered the intimidation factor and left the host feeling relieved: "You're kinda moving the needle with me."

I continued: "Because I'm out there having *conversations* on LinkedIn or YouTube, I get calls to appear on podcasts, requests to speak at conferences, and hired to coach individuals and teams. I'm not selling. I am sharing my experiences and thoughts about public speaking. I am simply having meaningful conversations."

"I'm really, really intrigued with the conversational approach," the second host chimed in. "This reframes a lot of things. Shelley, you've gotten us excited and I think, for that, you have fully succeeded in your challenge today!"

By sharing my experiences, I offered the hosts and their audience a different perspective on social media—that, between the cat memes and advertisements, it can be an incremental step to activating conversations that you care about. With each post you comment on, you're sharing something that is meaningful to you. You can listen to the full podcast episode, "How Solopreneurs Can Fall in Love With Using Social Media," from the Remarkable Framework playlist on my YouTube channel at youtube.com/@remarkablespeaking. I've also included the episode hyperlink in the Videos: How-To and More section of the workbook.

Conversations don't guarantee that people will connect with you. You can't control how someone responds to what you have to say. You have no idea if they have had a bad day or why they feel the way that they feel.

But this shouldn't stop you. Even the most successful communicators have rough patches in their speeches. When that happens, take a breath and channel that energy into excitement. Be curious to explore others' points of view. Then surrender the outcome, and a new opportunity to align with your audience will present itself.

If social media can be a conversation, just imagine what video can do! Next, you'll learn how video can change the way you do business.

Video Is Just Another Conversation

Smile for the camera!

Are you guilty of doing that with your phone—smile, click, and send? With all those photos stockpiling, what's holding you back from recording a video? It's just another conversation.

Why write an email or text when you can say it with a video? You'll get a stronger response when people see you because they will feel like they are interacting directly with you. Did you know that sending a video with your email or in-app messenger will improve your response rate by sixty percent? Video interactions boost viewers' retention by fifty-three percent more than plain text or infographics.[22] When all is said and done, speaking your message is three times faster to convey and results in fewer errors than typing.[23]

Recordings are a high-value relationship-building tool and another low-risk way to build your speaking skills. And the best part is that you don't need a big production setup to make them.

Back in Chapter 3's Your Blooper Reel subchapter, I alluded to the power of authentic versus perfect videos. Perfectionism can fuel anxiety by demanding a flawless performance, which is simply unrealistic. I should know—I failed at perfection. I feared that I was not good enough. And the endless revisions to attain perfection overshadowed my message. I had to remember how to let close enough be good enough.

After cutting my teeth at Ringling Bros. and Barnum & Bailey Circus, I landed the coveted job of assistant to Theoni Aldridge, the Tony Award-winning designer for shows like *A Chorus Line*, *Annie*, *42nd Street*, *La Cage aux Folles*, and *Dreamgirls*.

My first show with Theoni was the National Road Tour of *La Cage aux Folles*. The costumes were lavishly made of hand-painted silks, Swarovski crystals, and feathers from Paris. Every stitch, every sequin was deliberate, making every character's costume as unique as the character itself. My job was to see that the research and materials needed to construct the costumes were accurate.

It was opening night, and I was running in circles with a long list of to-dos. Renato's shoes had been dyed the wrong color; Albin's cape lining was two and a half inches too long; and there was a dancer who needed a last-minute costume fitting to understudy one of the Les Cagelles. There was no way I could have everything corrected and ready for the 8:00 p.m. curtain call. Theoni pulled me aside and said, "When that curtain goes up, Shelley can't be standing center stage sewing the buttons on Zaza's dress. What you've done is good enough."

In other words, the show must go on!

Don't let perfection be another excuse holding you back. You're here to become an excellent speaker, not a perfect speaker, and it just so happens that video is one of your most accessible, authentic opportunities to speak.

> Speak your mind—even if your voice shakes.
>
> —Maggie Kuhn

I have posted many videos on my channel that are far from perfect. I can complain that I look tired, my hair is out of place, or I flubbed my words, but these videos are out there in the YouTube universe, and that's what's important! You can listen to them for yourself on my YouTube channel at youtube.com/@remarkablespeaking.

As imperfect as some of my videos are, the comments have been positive. Viewers found my words inspiring. Some have hired me to speak at their conferences, and others booked me to lead a series of cohorts for speaker training. And there was one person who messaged me to say that she could not see my eyes because of the glare on my glasses. Aside from that good piece of advice, the show went on—and it is still running.

With the feedback, I am improving my production values, but not too much. The point is that I need to get it done and not wait for perfection before I do so.

When creating content now, I take a page from the playbook on how I approached internet marketing in the early 2000s: "Look what I can do," not "This is how I do it." Back then, as a marketer, I was sending emails at a time when only fifty-one percent of the population in the United States had a home computer and internet access,[24] a website was a standalone web page, and MySpace was this cool experience where you could chat with musicians. Internet marketers were writing the playbook in real time because social media didn't exist yet.

Reframing your self-talk to a "look-what-can-I-do" mindset to record videos is another opportunity for you to speak. I encourage you to always, whenever possible, send a recording in an email, text, or direct message, and notice the response when people experience *you*.

Don't know what to say? To find out how you can record a video message in seconds, use the sample worksheet that follows, and for a demo, go to the Remarkable Framework playlist at youtube.com/@remarkablespeaking. Both can be found in the workbook in the Videos: How-To and More section.

ONE-TAKE VIDEO MESSAGE WORKSHEET	
Message 1	
Message 2	
Message 3	

Choose an email or text that you need to respond to.

STEP 1) Set a timer for thirty seconds and say—out loud—your one big idea that you want the other person to know.

STEP 2) Write a brief descriptor on the One-Take Video Message worksheet.

STEP 3) Set a timer for sixty seconds and record your message using your favorite video app.

STEP 4) Post it, share it, send it! It's that fast.

Recording videos does not have to be time consuming—and they are definitely not going to be perfect! There are times when you'll need a beautifully produced video, but this is not one of them.

What you need to know to improve on-camera confidence:

- If you're distracted by looking at yourself on the screen, turn off your self-view when you're recording. Since you don't look at yourself when you're physically in a room with people, I recommend turning off your self-view for any online event. Speak into the camera lens or look at the people on your screen and put yourself in the digital room.
- If you feel like you're speaking too fast, manage your energy with a few breaths to slow down into calming confidence.
- If you make a mistake, don't overthink it. You're here to improve your speaking skills; and with all those emails you have to reply to, there will be plenty of opportunities to record.
- If you want to engage your audience, before you speak into the camera, ask yourself, "How do I feel about what I'm saying?" Let viewers know you care.
- Even if you feel uncomfortable, keep recording. With each recording, focus less on the not-so-good videos and be motivated by the good ones.

Here's my favorite hack I learned from a client who teaches a course on video production. You make a list of ten topics and record ten videos in ten minutes. For example, if you're responding to an email about a proposed agenda for an upcoming meeting, list ten key suggestions you'd like the group to consider. If you're creating content for how-to videos, list ten action items or pro tips. If you're pitching a prospect, list ten examples where customers have successfully used your product.

Once you have your list of ten topics, set a timer for one minute and record one topic from your list. Reset the timer for another minute and record a second topic, and continue recording one after the other without stopping. In ten minutes, you'll have ten recordings. Some will be good and some not so good. You might be surprised at how well you actually do. Maybe you get five good recordings, so repeat the exercise and get five more. Look for the Minute Content Creator worksheet in the Videos: How-To and More section of the workbook at remarkableframework.com.

MINUTE CONTENT CREATOR WORKSHEET	
Topic 1	
Topic 2	
Topic 3	
Topic 4	
Topic 5	
Topic 6	
Topic 7	
Topic 8	
Topic 9	
Topic 10	

The content creators I coach tell me that they no longer get hung up on trying to record the perfect take for their social channels, and this frees them up to have more time to level-up their creativity. Who knows—as a person who continues to raise the bar, you, like some of my clients, may be inspired beyond the scope of just making presentations, and, eventually, launch your own podcast or YouTube channel.

So grab your phone, laptop, or other favorite recording device, open the app, and hit record. Post it, share it, send it. Congratulate yourself on what you can do—you're out there, you're doing it, you're speaking remarkably!

Interject to Interact

Do you ever feel frustrated when someone in the meeting goes into rambling mode?

Picture this: It's that time of year when you bring your team together to do strategy planning or forecasting for the next quarter. Strategy sessions are meant to encourage everyone to share their ideas in an open forum. But the discussion can go sideways when one team member dominates the conversation and no one else gets the opportunity to speak.

Maybe that person is saying something interesting but they're just talking too fast. Or maybe they're simply droning on. You want them to stop rambling, but how do you do it in a way that doesn't sound rude?

You can politely interject with paraphrasing.

Paraphrasing is a very practical skill, commonly used as a strategy in negotiations and conflict resolution. You paraphrase when you repeat something that the person has said as your response. By acknowledging the person and what they've said, you show your interest, and they feel heard. You've quelled the rambling, created a moment for everyone to rest and digest, and maintained that person's participation in the conversation.

A great example of this technique is an interview on "The Treatment," an arts podcast by the NPR member station KCRW. Before you read on, listen to the forty-second audio clip where host Elvis Mitchell interjects to pause his guest, actress, writer, and producer Diarra Kilpatrick. You can find the audio clip, "An Example of Interjection," in the Remarkable Framework playlist on my YouTube channel at youtube.com/@remarkablespeaking and in the Videos: How-To and More section of the workbook.

Did you catch the moment of interjection? If not, listen again. It is easy to miss because Mitchell is so seamless that even his guest didn't notice. It's the moment when he says, "You were just getting at, I'm sorry I cut you off. I'm so excited to talk to you about living in two worlds at once, that [is what] the show is really about." The interjection became part of the discussion, and the host and guest happily continued their interview.

There also are those occasions where a side conversation takes the meeting off topic, and you find yourself wondering, "Is this ever going to end?" Maybe you have to take another call or go to another meeting. Is there an appropriate interjection for this situation? Absolutely. "You make a good point, but unfortunately we have to break for another meeting. Please, let's follow up by email" or "I want to dig deeper into that; can we revisit this later today to respect everyone's time for this meeting?"

It may feel uncomfortable the first time you interject. Like everything else, it takes practice. I was once facilitating a cohort with twenty-five people, and there was an individual, "Niccolò," who was rambling and not contributing much to the conversation. I interjected, but he resisted: "You're interrupting me, let me finish my point." I then offered, "I wanted to touch on something you mentioned earlier; it relates to the skill we are focusing on today," acknowledging what he had said. Niccolò was appreciative, quickly wrapped up his point, and the conversation moved forward. Shortly after, I received a few messages in the chat from other attendees thanking me for bringing the discussion back on topic.

When I led the next cohort, I asked the group for permission before the session started. "We want to cover a lot of good information today. May I get your permission to moderate and help to move things along for the sake of conserving time?"

As a speaker, facilitator, or moderator, it is your job to make the meeting a great experience. Interjection is a very powerful and effective tool when you want to keep it on topic and on time and is a valuable active listening skill. It puts a positive spin on someone who's dominating a conversation. When you interject by listening for something the person has said that you can relate to and then paraphrase it, you draw the person back into the original conversation. This lets them know that you appreciate their contributions. Interjection is a polite way to move things forward. When you interject with intention and kindness, people understand that you're interested in what they're saying, they are being heard, and that you care.

When you're moderating a discussion, try interjecting with these speaking prompts to share enthusiasm, add value to what someone is saying, and introduce another perspective to the conversation. You can find more in the Speaking Prompts section of the workbook at remarkableframework.com.

- "I agree with (name of person interrupting), and I'd also like to add …"
- "I hadn't thought of that, and it brings me to another point …"
- "Hold that thought (name of person interrupting). I'd love to know if the group is interested in learning more about this idea."
- "What you're saying is really interesting, but I have another call. May we continue the discussion this afternoon?"

PRO TIP: A conversation is best when it flows! Interject and move the conversation to someone else to add another point of view.

Interjection is good for podcasts, panel discussions, sales and contract negotiations, and even social situations. Practice interjecting and hone your active listening skills. You'll keep people engaged with more meaningful conversations.

Now, turn your attention to situations when the crowd feels too large for small conversations.

If the Crowd Is Too Big, Make the Room Smaller

I hear this a lot: "I'm comfortable speaking with a couple of people, but when I get in front of a big audience, I fall apart and anxiety takes over!"

Does size really matter?

According to *Merriam-Webster*, the definition of public speaking is "the act or process of making speeches to a live audience" or "the art of effective oral communication with an audience." It seems like a live audience of one or two or ten or even five hundred people all qualify.

If you approach public speaking from the dictionary's definition, then you're speaking publicly everyday, whether you're chatting with a friend or leading a retreat for an entire company.

You are a speaker. You speak at home, at restaurants, or at the gym. You speak at the office with clients and colleagues. You speak in meetings, at conferences, and on podcasts.

This is the part where you resist. "But if only the room wasn't so big." Let me ask you this: Do you feel more anxious sitting or standing when speaking to a group? When you're giving a presentation in person or on Zoom? How about during an interview or leading a meeting in the conference room?

All these excuses about the room size, being on Zoom, or standing when presenting are no different than what color socks you're wearing. Yes, there are aspects of your environment that are relevant when you're speaking, but they're not an excuse to not talk. The show must go on.

You'll be in situations speaking one-to-one, one-to-many, one-to-any. It's not the size of your audience, it's what you believe. Do you believe you have the experience and credentials to talk about your journey? Your company? Your line of work?

You've got the job. If you believe that you're qualified to fill your role, then you can eliminate audience size, in-person or online, and any other excuses. You speak all day long.

Just like talking to people before your speech or workshop begins helps you overcome your fear of not having anything valuable to say, it also helps make the room smaller. As they arrive, use those icebreakers from Chapter 2 to greet them, encouraging conversation and networking. Involving people in the conversation brings a familiarity and comfort to *everyone* in the room, whether in-person, online, or a hybrid of both.

One of my favorite ways to lighten the load of carrying a conversation, as well as getting others involved in it, is a technique I call the Hand Off. This is where you hand off a question to someone in the group and they take the conversation from there.

For example, "Kitt, would you like to start us off today?" "Angela brings up a good point. Rishi, I know you had a similar breakthrough, would you share your findings with the group?" Followed by, "Serge, was there something you wanted to add before we move on?"

You're inviting people to join the discussion and acknowledging their contributions. That's when conversations start to feel more like collaborations.

It's not about size, despite what you hear. When you bring people into the conversation, the environment is less of a concern. Hopefully you are starting to realize that you have been comfortably speaking on stages all along. Further activating your speaking will take you to bigger stages than you ever imagined.

When you list your key takeaways to activate your speaking in Chapter 10 on page 180, be sure to also give yourself grace and a pat on the back for all the good things you are doing to improve your speaking so far.

Don't stop here! The journey to excellence continues in Chapter 5 where I introduce the new drills from the Framework that reveal your unfair advantage.

CHAPTER 5
REFLECT AND REVEAL

The Power of Prose

Humans have told stories since the beginning of time—over the millennia and across different languages and cultures. The earliest evidence of storytelling dates back to cave drawings in Lascaux and Chavaux, France, some thirty thousand years ago. Storytelling has evolved from drawings to poems, songs, books, and movies.

Human beings are drawn to the hero's journey, where Wonder Woman, Forrest Gump, and even James Bond have moments that reveal their flaws. You connect to song lyrics as the soundtrack for the cherished memories that you share. You reflect on poems and proverbs to enhance the meaning of your own experiences.

Your life's story is what makes you memorable beyond your job title or a label. That's why stories are a powerful speaking tool. I get it, not everyone feels like they're a great storyteller. But if it feels natural to talk about your experiences with friends and family, then, remember, you're telling stories all the time. Stories are how people click with you and relate to your personal journey.

If you're struggling because you can't think of anything to talk about, I've got a tool in the Remarkable Framework that helps you find stories everywhere. And I mean everywhere!

It's called a story bank. A story bank is a collection of interchangeable stories like your mic-drop moments, your lived experiences, examples that you've read, anecdotes you've heard, quotes you like, relevant case studies, or industry news that someone told you about.

These narratives are the content that you can use for any speaking situation like a speech or sales pitch. I'll show you how to choose the right content for your speaking event when you create an actual presentation in Chapter 7. For now, go to remarkableframework.com or scan the QR code, then go to the Story Bank section in the workbook and start banking content! A sample Story Bank worksheet follows.

STORY BANK WORKSHEET	
Story 1	
Story 2	
Story 3	
Story 4	
Story 5	
Story 6	
Story 7	
Story 8	
Story 9	
Story 10	

For this drill, I want you to reflect on what you've experienced in the last twenty-four hours. Those moments can be significant—you signed a new client—or something more mundane, like how you made the perfect poached egg for breakfast. Whatever it is, it doesn't matter. Comedian Jerry Seinfeld gave television audiences a lot to talk about with a show about nothing, so I bet there's a lot of nothing happening in your life too!

Set a timer for one minute and make a list of your moments using the Story Bank worksheet in the workbook. Your experiences don't have to be revolutionary, just random things that come to mind. Don't write them out in detail, simply make a list using brief descriptors. For example:

- Quarterly review with board of directors.
- Met a friend for lunch.
- Software implementation for the finance department.
- I broke my favorite sunglasses.

If you're still writing after one minute, great. If you couldn't think of anything, take another minute and repeat the drill. If you listed three moments, congratulations, you have three moments deposited into your story bank! You'll continue to the next drill with those three stories.

Since this is a journey to remarkable speaking, it's time to talk about your moments. And talking about your moments is best understood when spoken in everyday language.

The greatest orators and storytellers—from Barack Obama to Harper Lee—do not rely on taglines and bullet points. They communicate in natural, everyday language known as prose. The Latin root of prose, "prosa oratio," means "straightforward or direct speech." If you want to connect with your audience, you must be straightforward and speak like yourself.

Think of when you are telling friends about a fun time. You're revealing a particular moment as you reflect on it; the experience, as you tell it, unfolds organically, like an anecdote. You're not worried about applying any formal structure to your tale. But as soon as your moment, your experience, becomes part of a speech, you might find yourself tempted to make it more formal, to structure it into the traditional "story" with all the proper elements—exposition, action, conflict, denouement, conclusion. No longer are you casually recounting the moment as it happened. If your brain is focused on building a three-story scaffolding—beginning, middle, and end—for a story about the last meal you ate, it's no surprise that you'll get stuck rambling in thought, with your words tumbling out of your mouth uncontrollably. Or your mind draws a blank. And there is nothing straightforward or direct about that!

So I encourage you to think of your moments and experiences instead of stories for this drill to avoid falling into the trap of trying to "write a story in your head." When you talk about your experiences as you remember them, you free your mind from structure, you speak naturally with feelings and without hesitation, and you're never at a loss for words.

Choose one of the moments from your worksheet. Set a timer for one minute and start talking about it. Speak like yourself as you recall it happening. Remember, you're not acting a part or reading an annual report. You are speaking as if you're having a conversation. Go with the first thought and don't overthink it. If you get stuck, do the Power Up drill.

Now choose another moment for your next one-minute talk. As you reflect on each moment, you'll realize that they are not so mundane afterall. You now know how much people love stories, so start speaking about yours!

PRO TIP: Use "I," "me," or "my" language to make it specific to your experience versus speaking in vague references such as "you" or "we." Lead off your one-minute talk with one of these "I" prompts. You'll find a full list in the Speaking Prompts section of the workbook at remarkableframework.com.

- There was a time when I ...
- I remember the moment ...
- I once had to ...
- Something unexpected happened when I ...

This minute drill has given you a story bank of at least three moments that are top-of-mind for you to use in your next introduction or networking meet and greet. Do you see what's happening? You're finding moments everywhere. Moreover, those moments do not have to be something that happened to you per se; they can be stories that you heard about from a colleague or read about in industry trades. Whatever the situation, you experienced it in some form.

At first, it may feel uncomfortable when no one else is making introductions in this way. It's something new, and, over time, you'll start to see how people take notice and click with what you're saying.

At this point you're doing plenty of drill repetitions to improve your speaking; and building a story bank as part of this routine will give you plenty of things to talk about without getting tongue-tied.

Sidestepping the scaffolding when telling stories is a great start. Next, you'll discover how tapping into the hidden details makes your stories captivating and memorable.

The Devil Is in the Details

Now that you have a collection of moments on your Story Bank worksheet, it's time to get specific.

It's a strain on your brain when you try to summarize and theorize in real time. You struggle to figure out the perfect words to say and end up rambling. Like I discussed in the previous subchapter, if you describe your experiences as you remember them happening, you'll find it easier to access your words and speak like yourself. When you do this, you speak more spontaneously because you're recalling moments using your senses, just like when you speak in casual conversations.

And it allows you to go into detail. Getting specific is the difference between reading Shakespeare in its entirety and skimming a summary. If you're merely summarizing Shakespeare, can you really feel the impassioned love between Romeo and Juliet or sense the rage of Macbeth's wrathful ambition?

A summary gives you an overview, but you don't get any of the expressive details that help you connect with the character's unique qualities. When you're speaking, making a point to be specific about your experiences adds nuance and uniqueness that reveal your authenticity. It is difficult to come across as authentic when you're summarizing.

Journalist and biographer Robert Caro is renowned for his research methods of extensive and immersive exploration into the world of his subjects, drawing readers into the heart of the story.

In his book *The Path to Power*, Caro chronicles Lyndon B. Johnson's ascent from humble Texas roots to one of the most powerful figures in American history.[25] In his research for the book, Caro went to Texas to meet with LBJ's brother, Sam Houston Johnson, to truly understand the life that shaped the thirty-sixth president of the United States.

A recount of that Texas visit was filmed by Lizzie Gottlieb in her documentary *Turn Every Page*, which documents the fifty-year relationship between Caro and his editor. Lizzy shared her firsthand account of what she experienced in a radio interview that would later become a major scene in the film:[26]

> *Going with Robert Caro to the Texas Hill Country was probably one of the most magical experiences of my life. We went into LBJ's boyhood home, and I sat there with Robert Caro in the house that Johnson grew up in. And Caro tells a story in the film sitting in that house about when he got Sam Houston Johnson, Lyndon Johnson's brother, to come back to the house that they had grown up in, and*

> *to sit there at dinner time with the shadows coming into the room the way they had when they were kids. And he somehow gets Sam Houston Johnson to open up and say things that he had never said before about their childhood and about Lyndon's very difficult, very painful relationship with his father. So Bob Caro pulls this story, the sort of untold story out of Sam Houston Johnson. That reveals something about how Lyndon Johnson became this unusual president that he became. And I got to sit there with Bob Caro in the same space, with the same shadows coming into the room and have him relive that experience himself. It was an incredible kind of life changing thing for me to be there.*

When you let yourself explore your moments and experiences, wandering and revealing specific details in the same way Sam Houston Johnson did, you're taking your audience on the journey with you. A single moment can express great wisdom, heartfelt empathy, creativity, and maybe even a little humor. There's no searching outward; when you're speaking, you must look inward.

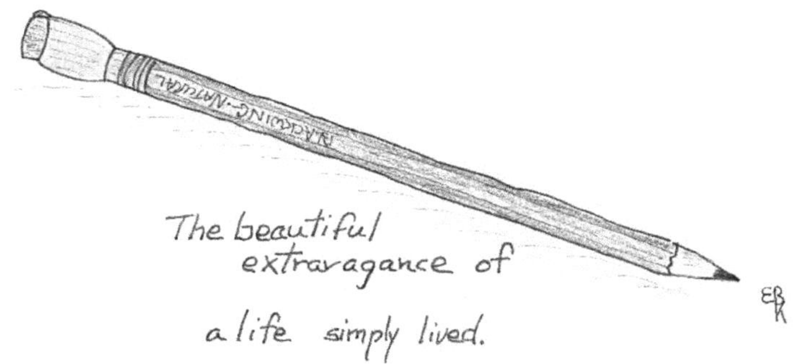
The beautiful
extravagance of
a life simply lived.

I experienced inward reflection with a technique I learned from a meditation workshop led by mindfulness-based psychotherapist Roger Nolan some twenty years ago. My clients know it as the Cranberry Effect.

Roger handed each person in the class one dried cranberry. He then set a timer for five minutes and asked us to observe the cranberry. I remember thinking, "I gave up my afternoon to stare at a cranberry?" But I was there to learn, so I reluctantly gazed at the tiny dried piece of fruit. I noticed dark shades of red and purple-brownish colors. I also saw different textures and shapes.

Okay, I had done it, but Roger then set a timer for fifteen minutes and asked us to continue observing. I was frustrated, wanting to know where this was going, but the longer I observed, the more lost I found myself in that little cranberry. My mind took me to a Thanksgiving dinner. I was cooking fresh cranberries in a pot with sugar and orange slices. The cranberries started to pop, and the syrupy mixture turned a beautiful shade of ruby red. Suddenly I heard a plop. My cousin had opened the oven door to baste the turkey. Then, in slow motion, we watched as an eighteen-pound turkey dropped out of the oven and slid across the kitchen floor, trailing an oil slick behind. The oven shelf had collapsed. With no way to use the oven, my cousin and I scrambled to cook this bird behemoth on the barbecue—all while keeping a hungry mob entertained amidst the chaos. It was through those details that I remembered how grateful I was for a feast that almost didn't happen!

What else did I see? I thought about a hike I took with some friends. We'd decided to take a detour to an overlook, which added another two miles at the end of the six mile loop. We stayed a little too long admiring the breathtaking panoramic views. On the way back, we had to navigate through overgrowth that blocked the not-so-well-used trail. It was getting dark, and we were getting hungry. One friend had a few bites leftover from his sandwich, and I had a bag of trail mix. The sandwich was soggy, and the mix, unfortunately, was a mushy blob of cranberries, nuts, and melted chocolate. We ate it anyway! An hour later, we approached the trailhead covered in brush and mud. There was another group having a picnic, and they invited us to join. My friend turned to me and said on that day and on every day we hiked thereafter: "It doesn't get any better than this."

"Times up!" Roger called out. Startled by his warning, I realized this cranberry had me in a trance. The more I let myself wander, the more details I remembered.

With details, these simple, ordinary stories evolved to be extraordinary. They are good examples of how I understand the meaning of the phrase "the devil is in the details." Now it's time for you to wander in the details. When you experience the Cranberry Effect using the following steps, you need to get very specific to get into the moment. I have also created a video to guide you through the Cranberry Effect. The hyperlink is accessible in the Cranberry Effect section of the workbook and on the Remarkable Framework playlist at youtube.com/@remarkablespeaking.

Get seated in a comfortable position on the floor or in a chair. Pick up an object that's in your current surroundings. It can be anything, a pen, your computer mouse, or a pair of glasses. Set a timer for five minutes. Next, look at the object and observe. Really study it carefully, looking closely at the details.

What do you see?

Why do you have this object?

When did you last use it?

What was happening at that moment?

Keep looking. What else do you see?

As you reflect on these details, perhaps you begin to think of moments that you haven't thought of in a long time, and, surprisingly, they come flooding back to your memory. These are the visceral qualities I want you to reveal when you're looking at the object. Ask yourself these questions, and let your mind wander.

> **PRO TIP:** Don't summarize because the details help to tell the story and explain your point.

> **PRO TIP:** Use the "I" prompts to bypass the story structure.

> **PRO TIP:** Tap into your bodily senses to revisit the moment experientially. Can you visualize the room? Do you smell the aromas? What sounds do you hear? What kind of movements are you experiencing? Was there a sweetness to the taste or a texture to the touch that prompts you to reveal the moment?

If you are stuck in your head and overthinking, do a few tongue twisters and take that breath. Getting lost in the details is another way to free your mind from being tongue-tied with nothing to say.

> What matters in life is not what happens to you
> but what you remember and how you remember it.
>
> —Gabriel García Márquez

You now have a story bank of moments from the most recent twenty-four hours of your life. But that's not the only place where you can find stories. You'll discover in the next subchapter that it's also what you know.

Start With What You Know

No one has your experience, period.

If you're speaking to a group of business owners who just raised capital, every owner will have a different experience. Every single one.

What about your work makes you an expert? Is it the way you discovered your market niche, or how many deals you've made, or what initiatives you implemented to grow the company?

When you reflect on the moment you founded your company or how you led the takeover of another organization, you begin to realize just how unique those moments are to you and how much they reveal about your distinctive characteristics. When you talk about what you know, people will be able to understand your thinking process. Your story sheds light on what kind of leader you are and builds your credibility.

I coached "Roy," an entrepreneur, right after he sold his business for hundreds of millions of dollars. He was approached to speak on panels and podcasts but turned the opportunities down. A college dropout, he had built a hugely successful global brand from the ground up. However, the enterprising entrepreneur was not comfortable talking about his success because he felt a void. He said when the company was sold, it felt like his identity was sold with it, and he had nothing interesting to say.

You can sometimes feel disconnected from what you've done in the past. But here's the thing: All those experiences you've encountered on your journey, at work and at home, add up to become the distinctive characteristics that shape your unique identity. Every success, every challenge, every lesson learned is part of your unique journey. If my client didn't talk about his successes, who would?

Using the Remarkable Framework during my coaching, Roy and I worked together to rediscover his mic-drop moments to add to his story bank. The entrepreneur quickly realized his experiences were not stuck in a past life—they revealed a lot about the life he was living currently.

The character Paul Hunham from the movie *The Holdovers* sums it up best: "Before you dismiss something as boring or irrelevant, remember, if you truly want to understand the present or yourself, you must begin in the past. You see, history is not simply the study of the past. It is an explanation of the present."

Memories from your past are stored in your temporal lobe, your knowledge base. It's what you remember and what you know. As you add content to your story bank in this next drill, you will tap into your knowledge base and rediscover your lifetime of mic-drop moments.

Open your workbook, found at remarkableframework.com, to the I AM section. Set a timer for two minutes and, on the I AM worksheet, write out the entire statement that follows, listing as many successes as you can. Don't hold back. Your work is routine, you're very skilled at what you do, and it's true, so you can write without judgment.

I am good at ____________ because I succeeded at ____________.

For example:
I am good at *coaching executives* because I succeeded at *listening to what they are not saying to help them achieve their speaking potential*.

How did it feel to write out your successes? Pretty good, right?

Take a few seconds and reflect on the very moment you experienced one of your successes.

Take another few seconds and reflect on how that moment influenced your decision making today.

Next, speak each success statement out loud.

Speaking each success out loud probably sounds and feels better than good. Own it. These are, after all, your unique experiences. They reveal your distinctive characteristics. If you sell the company or leave the job or a customer quits, you take your experiences and characteristics with you. That is your X factor.

Now add your successes to your Story Bank worksheet.

> Your story is what you have, what you will always have. It is something to own.
>
> —Michelle Obama

New research suggests that sharing good news benefits people through what researchers call capitalizing on positive events.[27] When you talk about good news, including others' successes (and feel genuinely happy for them), people get excited and they feel gratitude and a closer bond with you. And you, as the one sharing, feel happier and grateful just the same. There is evidence that even in some cultures where sharing personal successes can be frowned upon as "boastful," individuals are nonetheless motivated to share when they feel recognized, validated, and cared for. "The results suggest that we should be sharing positive events, but also try to encourage other people to share good events with us, so that we can give them those positive responses," says study coauthor Alexandra Gray.[28]

Knowing what you know also means being very honest about what you don't know. Think of those times when someone asks you a question and you don't have a clue how to answer it. You can embrace not knowing and respond with "Thank you for bringing this to my attention. I don't have the right answer right now, but I will check with the team and get back to you. Here's what I do know ..."

Not knowing something is not a weakness, it's a sign of confidence. So is, "I don't understand," "Can you please explain more," and "What a great question, let me give that some thought."

When you're honest about not knowing something, you become more trustworthy, and deeper conversations will emerge from that place. But if you say something that's not accurate, or you make something up to avoid being seen as someone who doesn't have all the answers, you discredit yourself and your confidence along with it.

Acknowledging what you don't know
is the dawning of wisdom.

—Charlie Munger

No one knows everything. You know something. Talk about what you know.

You're feeling comfortable talking about what you know and your successes. Now move forward and get comfortable talking about the learning moments from when you failed because revealing your failures may be your most remarkable quality.

Fail Forward

You feared speaking. You're now speaking up.

You feared you'd say the wrong thing. You're now asking questions and starting conversations.

You fear failure. You will now embody failure as your hero's journey to success.

Failure is nothing shameful. It even has its own museum. The Museum of Failure recognizes the products and ideas discarded along the way to innovation.[29] The mobile museum, which travels around the globe, was founded in 2017 by psychologist Dr. Samuel West to "Help people recognize that we need to accept failure if we want progress."

When you have greater responsibility, failure feels uncomfortable because of the unrealistic expectation that, as a leader, you are infallible and always make the right call. Failure can leave you feeling powerless, with a loss of control in challenging situations that risks damaging your credibility. But failure is a necessary step on the journey to being a resilient and effective leader.

By openly discussing your own moments of failure and how you learned from them, you can help others see failure as a temporary setback, not a permanent roadblock. When you lead with compassion from a growth mindset, you motivate teams to persevere.

Dr. West relates failure back to the value of stories. "One thing all failures have in common is a story. A story we can learn from." Are you—the leader, that person who persevered, the one who stopped at nothing to get where they are today—are you talking about your stories of failure that led to your successes?

One of the biggest failures at 3M led to one of their biggest successes. Spencer Silver was a chemist at 3M on the research team assigned to develop a strong adhesive glue. But the glue was only mildly adhesive, and the team abandoned the failed product.

But Silver discovered something in the adhesive called microspheres which allowed the adhesive to slightly stick and peel easily from surfaces without leaving residue. Although frustrated that his fellow chemists paid no attention to this, he believed in its possible applications and continued experimenting with the adhesive and speaking about the not-so-sticky idea at conferences and seminars.

Another 3M scientist, Art Fry, was frustrated but for a different reason. A singer in his church choir, Fry organized his singing notes by inserting small pieces of paper between the pages of the hymnal only to find that the loose paper notes would usually fall out.

Fry was in the audience when Silver gave his talk on microspheres and wondered if the mild adhesive could be used to stick his notes in place without damaging the hymnal.

Silver and Fry partnered up to further develop the product. Coworkers soon started using the sticky notes to communicate around the office, and Post-it®[30] became 3M's billion-dollar failure.

> Fail early, fail often, but always fail forward.
>
> —John C. Maxwell

Now I'd like you to make a list of what you're good at today because of how you failed at something in the past and add it to your story bank. This is you reframing failure into a learning moment.

Go back to the I AM section of the workbook and set a timer for two minutes. This time, write out the entire statement that follows about the things you have failed at. List as many failures as you can. By identifying your failures, you will have more things to talk about in those situations when someone catches you off guard with a challenging question. The more you do this drill, the more clear and concise your speaking will be because, as a leader, you can demonstrate the value of learning from your mistakes while creating a safe space for others to learn without judgment.

I am good at ______________ because I failed at ________________.

For example:
I am good at *recording authentic videos in minutes* because I failed at *trying to make a perfectly scripted video*.

If you feel like you're falling back into old habits, like getting stuck in your head, judging, and doubting yourself, take a few minutes to do the Power Up drill to reframe your selfish self-talk.

How did it feel to write out your failures?

Take a few seconds and reflect on the very moment you experienced one of your failures.

Take another few seconds and reflect on how that moment influenced your leadership style today.

Next, speak each failure statement out loud.

Own it and add these statements to your Story Bank worksheet.

If you have tried and failed, you no doubt have a teachable story. It's not that you failed, because everyone experiences failure, it's that you learned something in the process and it wasn't the end of your journey. That's an exceptional quality and an intrinsic part of your success.

You're in the role you're in because of *how* you responded to failure. Failing forward can be a key factor in realizing your unfair advantage.

Your Unfair Advantage

Speakers around the world, the ones you listen to and follow, whether on YouTube, TikTok, or a podcast, often share some part of their journey with their audiences. Human beings are captivated by the hero's journey. People love their stories because as they mirror the speaker's experiences and reflect on their own, the brain's reward system triggers the feel-good hormone dopamine.

So what is your hero story? Start with your X factor. It may sound a little like comic-book hero stuff. And you're right! Your X factor is your distinctive characteristics that make you "comic-book hero" remarkable. Your X factor is unique to you, and that is your unfair advantage as a speaker, as a leader, and as a person.

You've likely heard of soft skills like active listening, critical thinking, and creativity. Also called people skills or interpersonal skills, these are personal attributes that help you interact with others. Your X factor is the *way* you communicate or *how* you think critically and *what* actually makes you creative. Unlike hard skills, which are specific to expertise like financial planning, Photoshop, or multilingualism, soft skills are difficult to measure. Yet you depend on them to define your relationships, and it's why people see you as influential.

According to research conducted by America Succeeds, skills like communication, critical thinking, and creativity are in high demand

and pivotal for all job types and levels.[31] The good news is that these skills are transferable.

That is how I navigated my career journey from costumes to marketing to becoming a public speaking coach. I learned hard skills, but it was my transferable soft skills that people noticed and that got me the job. I heard plenty of *nos* between the few *yeses*. The common factor among the *yeses* was that I shared moments that explained how I could offer a new perspective. That is why talking about your experiences is so important. People can see that you're a leader by your title, but they want to know *how* you lead. When you share your experiences, you lead by example.

Princess Diana was known as the people's princess. Her legacy endures because she lived what she advocated for. At a time when HIV/AIDS victims were considered outcasts and people to be avoided, she visited them in hospitals and treatment centers. Her landmine walks in Angola raised awareness for landmine victims, which led to the signing of the Ottawa Mine Ban Treaty to dismantle landmines globally. When she spoke about her work publicly, people described her as compassionate, humble, and accessible. Leading by example, Princess Diana revealed all those qualities without ever uttering those three words.

Just like when I told the Post-it® story, you understood that Silver and Fry were resilient and innovative without me describing them that way.

When you speak about the things you've done, people understand what kind of critical thinker and leader you are. You might think you're bragging, but sharing your journey is not bragging when it's true. You're not saying "I'm great," you're sharing a moment that shows how remarkably great you are. Collecting them in your story bank is like having a CV of your remarkable moments!

There are three and a half billion people employed worldwide,[32] and there's a good chance that many of them have your same job title. They may be great at building a company, but they don't have your critical eye. They may have found a solution to a similar problem, but they don't make decisions the way you do. They may be an enterprising leader, but they don't negotiate with your gravitas. Sharing your experiences gives context to what *you've* accomplished.

By now, you have plenty to talk about—interesting moments, successes, and failures. Continue speaking up and implementing the drills into your routine because it's going to transform the way you speak and lead.

Continue reflecting on your experiences to add more content to your Story Bank worksheet. Revealing specific moments will bring them to life because storytelling is the most efficient way to communicate your ideas and the most effective way to lead by example. Talking about your journey is your unfair advantage that will transcend your X factor beyond one speech.

> I don't think about art when I'm working.
> I try to think about life.
>
> —Jean-Michel Basquiat

This is a good time to reflect on your key takeaways in Chapter 10 on page 180.

After all this talking, let's turn the volume down. Way down. In Chapter 6, I'm going to ask you to stop speaking and keep quiet. Because sometimes the most powerful thing you can say is nothing at all.

CHAPTER 6
KEEP QUIET

Let the Silence Speak

The awkwardness that ensues when no one is speaking may only last a few seconds, but it can seem like it's going on forever. You might feel the need to keep talking every minute you are in conversation to ease the anxiety of silence. Maybe you feel pressure because you have a ton of information you want to share and the clock is ticking. "I've got to fill the space!" "I've got to make my point!" "I've got to tell them everything!"

No, you don't. It may seem counterintuitive, but keeping quiet and not talking is perhaps the most multipurpose skill you'll need to be a remarkable speaker. To begin with, the empty space that the silence creates brings focus to the words being spoken and allows for more impactful communication. This is how your audience is able to fully digest what you are saying.

This brings me to Rubin's Vase, an optical illusion created by contrasting black and white colors. The shape you see changes based on your perspective of which space is empty.

If the black is the empty space, how sharp is the white shape?

If the white is the empty space, how sharp is the black shape?

Could you say both the space and shape have equal focus? Just because one color may seem like empty space does not mean that the shape lacks definition.

The contrast with silence and speaking works the same way. The silence speaks volumes and enhances your words. In essence, the empty space helps to define the importance of your message.

One way to introduce silence into your speaking is to take a breath after you've made a statement to add emphasis, like an exclamation point! This will help create that sharp contrast.

Another way is to take a breath to create space when you make a mistake, and come back stronger with focus and clarity. Take a breath when you lose direction of what you're saying, creating space until inspiration resurfaces. The breath helps you to be more concise with your answers rather than rambling just to fill the silence, which will only confuse you and your audience more.

> **PRO TIP:** When you take a breath, count to four before you utter a word.

Breath is the connection between mind and body. You don't really think about breathing, it's second nature. But when you take conscious breaths, you can bring focus to your mind and put your body in the relaxed state that I talked about in Chapter 2. The more deliberate and deeper your breath, the higher the level of consciousness you can achieve, which opens space in your mind to new ways of thinking. In that space, you can ask yourself, "What's another perspective on this topic?"

> Breath is the bridge which connects life to consciousness, which unites your body to your thoughts. Whenever your mind becomes scattered, use your breath as the means to take hold of your mind again.
>
> —Thich Nhat Hanh

The greatest speakers that I've worked with and admire are those who are most comfortable creating space by not speaking. Just don't suck all the air out of the room.

Take Up Space Without Sucking Out the Air

People who talk a lot and take up space in a room are perceived as leaders. In a study about the babble hypothesis,[33] lead author Neil MacLaren said their research showed that "People seemed to attribute leadership to people who babbled" or who just spoke a lot. They babbled and rambled on and on (and you wonder why meetings are not as productive as they can be!).

I have encouraged you to speak up as often as possible because it's the best way to improve your speaking skills. However, you don't want to talk to just fill the air.

As a mid-level manager joining her senior leaders in the boardroom, Karen Lynch was told to "Sit in the back, not at the table, because women just take up space." From that moment forward, she did not hold back from sharing her purpose. She spoke up often, advocating for better healthcare and contributing to ideas in meetings. Years later, when she was named CEO of CVS Health®, Lynch wore a T-shirt on her first day in her new position that said, "Taking Up Space."

The shirt inspired her to write a book with the same name encouraging more women to take up space and talk about their experiences. *Fortune* gave Lynch space on their "50 Most Powerful Women in Business" list six years in a row and named her "Most Inspirational CEO." *Forbes* gave her space on their inaugural "50 Over 50" list, and *Bloomberg* thought she deserved space on their list as one of "50 People Who Have Changed Global Business."[34]

Taking space goes a long way, but you might be asking how long is the right amount of time to stay silent in that space?

As long as it needs to be.

Steve Jobs famously lingered in silence when he spoke and lingered in even longer pauses when someone asked him a question. I'm talking thirty seconds to a full minute. Jobs was a master of taking up space when he spoke, and no one ever left the room or stopped buying Apple products because of it. People were captivated by the suspense and perhaps felt more intrigued because they were sharing space with one of the great minds of the twenty-first century.

When, like Jobs, a speaker stops talking and takes space, it feels like a cliffhanger. And all of a sudden the silence isn't so terrifying. The people are drawn in ... what will the speaker say next?

The space can work like a magic eraser, eliminating the ums and ahs. (And if I bring any more attention to the ums and ahs, that's all you're going to worry about, and with an overflowing inbox, you've got more important things to focus on.)

But taking up space also can feel heavy, like dead air. In live broadcasting, dead air is a warning that something went wrong, like a technical issue. But for you, dead air will feel like pressure—pressure to speak.

So reframe the dead air as welcomed space. The silence is actually active because of all the good things happening. The space brings you back into focus, it brings clarity and significance to your words, and it gives your audience time to digest what you're saying. The space is anything but dead.

You want to keep the air in the room alive and flowing, and interjection can help you to move the conversation along if need be. But how do you know if anybody is actually listening? You're going to want to hear what I have to say next ...

You Hear Me, But Are You Listening?

According to Adam Grant, there are leaders who check their ego at the door because "The goal isn't to be the smartest person in the room; it's to make the entire room smarter."

You may have guessed from the previous subchapter that the person trying to be the smartest in the meeting is usually the person doing the babbling. So that would suggest the person actually making the room smarter is the one holding space, the one who listens to what is being said and makes sure every voice is heard.

As a social creature, you crave connection with others. Hearing words is one thing, but listening to engage and understand others' perspectives is how you elevate your ability to connect.

When active listening, you hold space by being attentive and reserving judgment. Rather than offer an opinion, you offer an understanding: "Did I get that right?" or "Is this what you mean?" Your understanding shows empathy and improves how you communicate. This is important for input and feedback, like one-on-ones or collaborations with teams.

Active listening works when you're speaking to larger audiences as well. If you have a keen awareness of what's happening in the room, you'll "hear" your audience tell you what they need. When I give presentations, I observe my audience's reaction in response to what I'm saying. I'll hold space by asking, "Are you still with me?" If they nod, I'll know that what I'm saying is resonating, and I'll nod back in agreement. If they signal *no* with a look of confusion, I'll ask more questions before moving on to my next point.

Being curious shows interest in others and also releases the pressure of having to do all the talking! As a speaker, you can bring your audience into the conversation by listening and sharing something of value in return. You'll learn about different perspectives that can potentially reshape your presentation for the better.

The more people feel heard, the more they feel respected and the deeper the connection. When that happens, instead of looking at their phones or turning away in boredom, they're interacting with you, and things start to click. Now that's smart!

Oprah Winfrey said all of her more than thirty thousand guests had one thing in common: They wanted to be heard. "What I started to hear was that people are really saying, 'Did you hear me?' and 'Did what I say mean anything to you?' I started to listen with that in mind, with that intention of validating that you're here, your speaking to me is important because you matter."

You've identified *your* successes in Chapter 5, now hold space for others and talk about theirs. "After seven months, I want to congratulate Arineh on the recent merger," and "Charley, I would like to know your perspective on last year's analytics." Let them know, "I am listening to you and might not be able to give you what you're asking for, but let's see how we can work together."

Your brain does some interesting things when someone else is talking. It can get stuck on one idea or one word they've said. While your brain is processing the meaning of that idea or word, it is also trying to listen to the new information as the speaker continues talking. With that kind of distraction, there's a good chance you'll miss part of what they're saying.

Have you ever witnessed an interview where the host stacks questions like an avalanche, asking several, one right after the other? The guest may have only heard the last question or got confused and digressed completely without answering any of the questions.

But if you hold space after asking a question or before you reply to their answer, you're allowing the brain time to process information. You're actively listening and showing thoughtfulness and consideration while acknowledging the importance of what they're saying. Listening helps you to develop a deeper understanding and build trusted relationships.

On the flip side, it can be challenging for others to listen to you if you're talking too fast. Like walking instead of running, there are some well-paced maneuvers you can do to slow down your speaking.

Walk, Don't Run

You finally got their attention and the floor is all yours. Why do you have the sudden urge to speak really fast and cram every bit of information into the conversation? Can that person even hear you let alone comprehend what you're saying?

In the age of the Internet of Things, consumption has greatly increased—consumption of both information and stuff.[35] Social platforms are designed to make you scroll, creating a sense of FOMO (fear of missing out) and a burst of adrenaline. The instant gratification you feel purchasing new stuff releases those happy hormones; but buyer beware, you'll crash and burn in the long run.

Similarly, when you're rushing to cram lots of information into your presentation, your fight-or-flight response triggers adrenaline just thinking about the vast amount of content you're delivering, so you talk faster. But the impact on your audience diminishes because they cannot effectively comprehend it all.

When you talk fast, you can come across as nervous, anxious, or even insincere.

When you rush, your words can sound muffled, making it difficult for people to understand you.

When you cram a lot of information into a short amount of time, you appear to be lecturing rather than having a conversation and sharing information.

It's better to cover one point really well instead of four points poorly. That is what I am doing here with you. I am coaching you to improve your speaking skills with an incremental approach one subchapter at a time. I want to give you space to practice and process each drill really well before you advance to the next stage.

If you want your audience to understand your message, talk at a slower pace to give yourself the space to explore your emotions and connect to your words. As a speaker, you don't want your audience to be in fight-or-flight trying to keep up with what you're saying. If you race through your presentation, you can't have an emotional connection to your story. If you feel pressured to get your speech over and done with or start rambling off on a tangent or notice your heart beating out of your chest, scan the audience for those glazed stares. If you see any, stop right there and take a breath. Give yourself space to reflect and savor the moment. Reflection brings you back to the present, and you will naturally speak slower and with more purpose, which will enable your audience to audibly receive your message.

One thing is certain: You will still get nervous at times. Journalist and news anchor Norah O'Donnell got the once-in-a-lifetime assignment to interview Pope Francis. Fellow journalist and morning news cohost Gayle King was astonished, "I have never seen you nervous, Norah. Never! I've worked with you for a long, long time. I can only imagine what this meant to you."

The news industry veteran confessed, "I was so nervous because I wanted to get it right, and I knew how important this was. I'm still nervous!" During her interview, O'Donnell, taking her time, shared her personal moments with Pope Francis. He acknowledged her empathy and responded with kindness, which helped her feel a little more comfortable and reduced the pressure to get it right.

When you talk slowly, your audience can follow your journey along with you. When you sense that you're speaking too fast, stop and take a breath and trigger the happy hormones that help you relax. After a pause, begin talking again using one of the following speaking prompts.

- On second thought, I'll say ...
- Let me break it down this way ...
- Before we take a deep dive, I want to share ...
- To put it more simply ...

For reference, you'll find a full list in the Speaking Prompts workbook section at remarkableframework.com.

Life goes fast, so walk, don't run, and, as they say, savor the moment.

Houston, We've Had a Problem

Apollo 13[36] was expected to be the third landing attempt on the moon. On day two of the flight, April 13, 1970, the three astronauts demonstrated what life and work was like in a weightless environment during a live television broadcast two hundred thousand miles back to Earth.

Nine minutes after the broadcast ended, the unexpected happened: There was an explosion. Command module pilot John "Jack" Swigert reported, "Houston, we've had a problem here."

Two oxygen tanks had blown up. With the warning lights blinking, the command module lost its normal supply of electricity, light, and water. Mission control in Houston did not have time to write and test new procedures; the clock was running out.

Panic and fear was not an option. The crew members managed to return the spaceship to Earth using only a piece of cardboard, a plastic bag, a hose from a pressure suit, duct tape, a sock, and their survival skills. The Apollo 13 space mission became known as "a successful failure."

Here on Earth, it's the pressure of high stakes that both motivates you and scares you as a leader. During the disruption in the supply chain caused by a global pandemic, your knowledge about industry resources and your resilience and innovation helped to create new products that generated greater consumer demand. You had to make tough staffing decisions as a result of the economic downturn during the housing market crash. Through your involvement in building the company from the ground up, you understood where to reduce overhead to streamline production, which yielded an increase in profit margins.

The adrenaline rush you experience during high-pressure situations is actually a good thing because you need that energy to motivate you when you speak. Your body feels the surge of energy, and when your brain recognizes that surge, you can choose to reframe what it senses as fear to excitement.

Because, by definition, it is not possible to practice public speaking by yourself in private, practice speaking in front of people and in as many different situations as you can. You need to replicate pressure to survive the unexpected. This is different from rehearsing a script. It's akin to astronauts practicing spacewalks in replica space modules submerged in gigantic pools of water to simulate the weightlessness of space. Or their constant training drills launching and landing the shuttle, recreating its thunderous noise and violent shaking within motion-based simulators.

Anything can happen during your talk and launch you into a fight-or-flight response. Take a breath, and shift into rest-and-digest to increase your resilience.

> **PRO TIP:** You have a new client meeting and discover your prospect is short on time and patience. Practice using the speaking prompts, and get to your point without rambling.
>
> **PRO TIP:** People arrive late during your talk, distracting your train of thought. Acknowledge their entrance, and reiterate a point you spoke about prior to the interruption.
>
> **PRO TIP:** There's an equipment failure, and you can't access your slide deck. Share a specific moment to paint a mental picture of the slide. As a backup, it never hurts to have a printed copy of your deck for reference.

The more you speak in public, the more you will not only survive adverse situations, you'll thrive.

Echoes Are Louder Than Words

The legendary talk show icon Larry King held space for his guests, "I never learned anything with my mouth open."

In the world of speaking, the silence is the rest. Everyone in the room needs a break, including you. Like an echo, the repetition of your words happens in the space of reflection between them.

> Technique is not music. Music is the thousandth of a millisecond between one note and another; how you get from one to the other—that's where the music is.
>
> —Isaac Stern

You're making progress from subchapter to subchapter with a steady routine of different speaking practices every day. Continue to build on that by adding new skills as well as reinforcing existing ones. Now make the most of the silence to echo what you've learned in a chapter review.

CHAPTER 1: Reframe your selfish self-talk, and get out of your head. Be curious and take the focus off of you. Build a routine to master the skills.

CHAPTER 2: Empower your beliefs, and take ownership. Breathe your nervous energy into calm. Make it a great experience, and look for opportunities to interact with people.

CHAPTER 3: Mic-drop moments will transcend people beyond your speech. Emotions are a good thing and give meaning to your words. Speak like yourself, mistakes and all.

CHAPTER 4: Activate, and have lots of conversations. Seek out *nos* as the fuel for motivation. Persevere, and find opportunities to speak.

CHAPTER 5: Reflect on and reveal your experiences. Get specific, and don't summarize. Lead by example, and let your X factor shine.

CHAPTER 6: Keep quiet, and create space. Let the silence bring focus and power to your words. Listen, and give your audience time to digest what you're saying.

Linger in the pause, and add your key takeaways for keeping quiet in Chapter 10 on page 181.

While practice is imperative, beware of overkill; straining your brain to learn new skills can actually make the process more stressful. Take a quick break—go for a walk, grab a coffee, or do a few cycles of box breathing, whatever works for you. So you don't forget, for your brain and your speaking, write the word BREATHE on a Post-it®, and stick it on your computer or at the top of your to-do list. Alternatively, download the following image from the BREATHE Post-it® section of your workbook at remarkableframework.com and use it as your screensaver.

Taking a breath is your all-around, good-at-anytime way to find calm. Your brain will recharge, and your speaking will have more clarity.

Chapter 7 is where it all comes together! The moment has arrived for you to use the Remarkable Framework to construct a full speech. It doesn't matter if you're doing a ten-minute pitch, a sixty-minute presentation, or a half-day immersion. With these tools, you'll be able to create a talk for any speaking opportunity, any audience, and any topic. The Framework is evergreen.

CHAPTER 7
ARTICULATE

See the Forest for the Trees

It can be hard and time-consuming to prepare for speaking events. They are so dynamic, and you have no idea what you're stepping into. The Remarkable Framework is a solution that gives you the confidence to speak in these situations with the support of reliable tools while eliminating the agony of lengthy drafts and writer's block.

The part of the Remarkable Framework discussed in this chapter is made up of the Shelley Grinder, the Tree Grid, and Evergreen tools. These tools are interconnected and work together to develop your speech. So when I refer to the Framework here, I mean all of these tools working in tandem as one solution.

The Shelley Grinder uses a combination of writing and speaking sprints much like the drills you learned in Chapter 5 to collect content for your story bank. The Shelley Grinder is a series of timed sprints that helps you to articulate both your key message and the supporting content for your talk, i.e., moments, experiences, examples, anecdotes, data, case studies, industry news, and so on.

Using the Tree Grid, you'll write down your key message, supporting content, and call to action for at-a-glance reference.

As a final step, the Framework's Evergreen is where you'll organize all the elements of the Tree Grid to structure your entire speech.

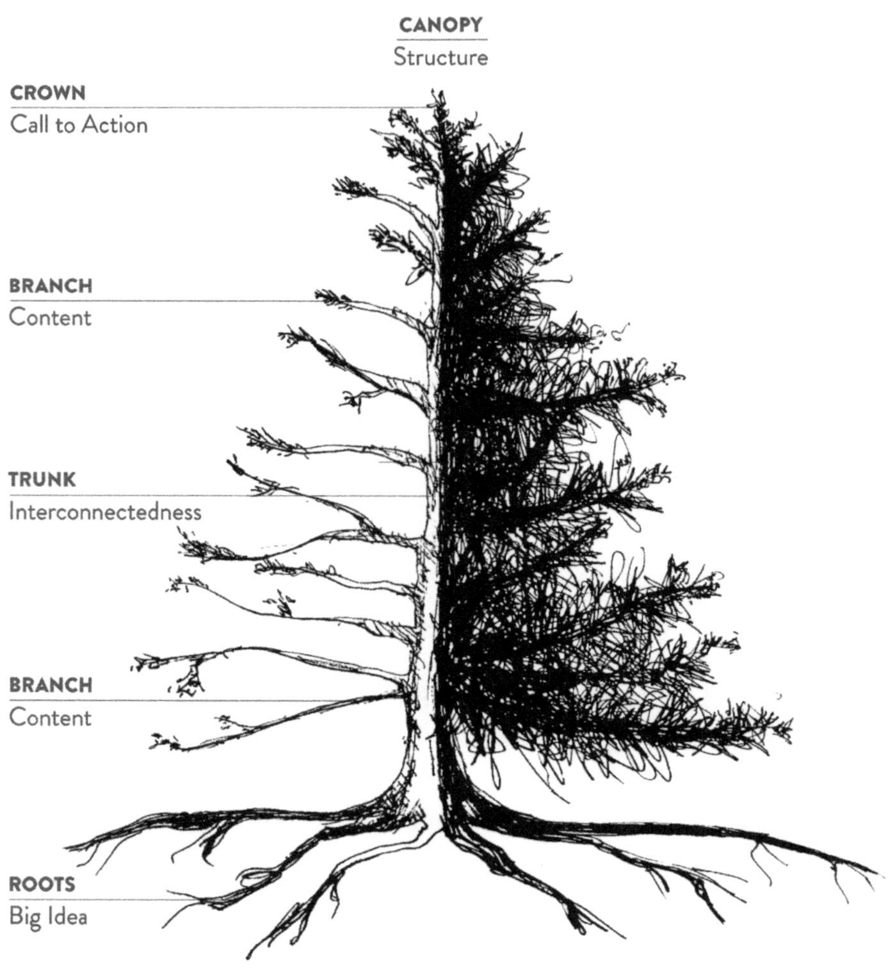

How does the structure of your speech resemble that of an evergreen? A tree symbolizes balance and harmony and the interconnectedness of everything. Starting with the root system of the Framework's Evergreen, your key message, or, as I call it in the Framework, your big idea, is the foundation of your speech. Firmly grounded, your big idea, like tree roots, needs to anchor the structure of your speech.

The trunk interconnects all the parts of the tree to balance the tree's structure. By repeating your big idea throughout your presentation, like a tree trunk, you reinforce the interconnectedness of all your supporting content. The repetition helps your audience to understand and retain your big idea. Repetition is recognition!

The branches of a tree are the lifelines that help to create the tree's canopy in the same way that your supporting content helps to explain your big idea. If a branch is broken, the dry stick is no longer useful to the tree. This is where you can remove unnecessary content and prevent cramming too much information into your talk. You can mix and match content from your story bank without hours of rewrites because, like branches of the tree, your content is interconnected to your big idea.

The crown that nurtures the Evergreen is the call to action that wraps up your speech. The call to action is an opportunity for you to nurture your audience to take action and stay connected, such as, "Download the Remarkable Framework at remarkableframework.com" or "Let's connect on linkedin.com/in/shelleygoldstein."

The canopy of the Evergreen reveals the tree's distinct shape, just like the structure of all the elements of your speech brings your big idea into clear view.

> To be without trees would, in the most literal way, to be without our roots.
>
> —Richard Mabey

Your audience shouldn't be confused before they're intrigued. The tools of the Remarkable Framework help you clarify your message, explore new perspectives, and position the content of your talk to adapt to any type and length of speaking event.

Let's say you've prepared for a forty-five minute presentation. The advisory board was delayed longer than expected, and they now only have twenty minutes to meet with you. Using the Evergreen, you can adjust the content without having to rewrite your entire presentation. As a matter of fact, there's very little writing because, using the Framework, at no point do you write an entire speech.

What's even more incredible about the Framework is that it is universal. You can create content, articulate what you want to say, and organize the structure for any speech, presentation, pitch, webinar, seminar, podcast, facilitation, meeting agenda, employee training, lunch and learn, panel discussion moderating, video recording, interview, social media post, toast, eulogy, and, yes, so much more!

Here's what clients had to say about using the Remarkable Framework for their speaking events.

"I was so surprised at how the Framework can be applied immediately and for so many different situations. My keynote and podcast and even social media; it's really amazing!"

"I appreciate your approach and guidance using the Framework to build my presentation deck. I'm going forward with more confidence now."

"I've done countless pitches for my company but un-pitching it with the Shelley Grinder was a quantum leap from what I'd been doing for years."

"Thank you so much for the Framework. This is exactly what I needed! It worked for my interviews, and I even used it to give a toast at my best friend's wedding!"

And this response from a client's client when she used the Framework to structure her webinar: "Wow!!! You knocked it out of the park for your very first one! I have some webinar spots to fill next quarter, and I could really use a strong speaker like you."

From roots to crown, you have the tools to develop the elements of your speech: your big idea, supporting content, and call to action. With its universal applications, the Remarkable Framework endures, standing the test of time. It's evergreen.

Bending Time for Speaking Mastery

When giving a talk, you want to find the golden mean between preparation and speaking in your natural voice. But the more time you spend thinking about the perfect words to say, the more you deplete your mental energy and the less focus you have for the talk itself. You lose sight of the forest for the trees.

In 2016, I was the marketing director for a rapidly growing sporting goods equipment manufacturer. My department was a small team of three people, and we had the herculean task of managing everything from content creation, social media, and email marketing to print collateral for catalogs, trade shows, and seminars to website development for over three hundred products, eight brands, and two divisions. We had software systems to help automate some workflows, but the team struggled to keep up with productivity. With a broad range of campaigns and demanding deadlines, my team was on the brink of burnout. Working harder wasn't going to make us more efficient; we needed to work smarter.

One intriguing way to work smarter is by compressing time, as Jake Knapp demonstrates in the book *Sprint*.[37] While working at Google Ventures, Knapp developed a five-day time-saving process to streamline Google's time-to-market pipeline by compressing months of development into a single week using sprints. Modeled after a runner running a short distance at full speed, sprints enabled teams to test different approaches, avoid costly missteps, and reduce prototyping before building a minimum viable product. John Zeratsky, a coauthor of *Sprint*, said about using sprints in work cycles, "It's not just about speed. It's also about momentum, focus, and confidence."

After finishing the book, I invited my team to a week of sprints to streamline and better manage productivity.

On the first day, the team met for an hour and worked in sprints to identify all the possible campaigns and document what hard skills each team member had, including skills outside of our job roles. For example, the marketing coordinator, who's primary role was managing the database and email funnels, revealed that he was Photoshop savvy. Learning each others' hard skills was critical because, as it turned out, each of us was capable, and willing, to utilize our secondary skills to avoid a bottleneck in production.

Day two, tracking time, the team prioritized the campaigns by their optimal ROI (return on investment). In addition, we discussed what assets were needed and how much time it would take to execute each campaign.

Day three, we organized an asset and template library from past campaigns and, where applicable, assigned them to current campaigns.

This was another time-saving step because it reduced the need to create content from scratch; instead, we repurposed social media posts and email funnels based on favorable performance metrics.

Day four, the team agreed on a roadmap for the overall marketing strategy. This final step of sprints ensured that the team operated as a cohesive unit, which resulted in a shared sense of ownership and achievement.

By huddling one hour a day for four days using sprints, the three of us created a process to identify what campaigns to focus on. Understanding our skill capabilities, we learned that any member of the team could produce an end-to-end campaign. This initiative is ideal for small teams because if one member is out of the office, the other two are able to keep the campaign moving forward to meet its scheduled deadline. With knowledge of high-performing assets, we storyboarded in the most efficient way possible—and didn't spend hours in development.

Sprints not only saved us time finding solutions to manage productivity and created a positive work culture, they made us smarter in how we used our time. My colleagues were blown away by the results: "Ask Shelley to do the impossible, and then she does the impossible!"

Fast-forward to 2020. As a newly certified coach for a public speaking startup, I was tasked to partner coach a skincare company's retail activation team. As I listened to the team of four present product demonstrations, I realized that the more time each person had to speak, the more they rambled on tangents and the less focused they became when communicating about the products.

I was curious: If I reduced their time speaking using sprints, would it create a path to clarity?

So I had one team member talk about her product for ninety seconds. Straight afterward, I asked her to repeat the demo, but I reduced the time to sixty seconds. Keeping the pressure on with a third round, I had her talk about the demo once again, only this time in thirty seconds. In three minutes, she was able to grind down her thoughts into one crystal clear idea!

I then repeated the same drill with the other three team members. When they gave their final demos, each member spoke for ninety seconds with focus, clearly articulating their experience with the product. Most surprising to them all? There were no signs of rambling or straying off topic with extraneous details.

My coaching partner was amazed! "You've really got something special here, Shelley." I was eager to test the drill for other types of work-related scenarios. Inspired, I designed a curriculum for professionals with different careers and from different industries. After spearheading thirteen cohorts of professionals, participants repeatedly were able to grind their thoughts and clearly articulate their ideas.

It turns out that, yes, using a drill of time-reduced, successive sprints, clients achieved clarity for presenting any idea for any situation. And the Shelley Grinder was coined by cohort participants who felt that they had *literally* been through a grinder!

Comparable to resolving complex solutions for business, I have found that using sprints for preparing speeches is one of the most efficient and fastest ways to hone your message, create content, and articulate your ideas with clarity—all without a script.

> A diamond earns its sparkle from the pressure it endures.
>
> —Matshona Dhliwayo

By reducing the time of each sprint and speaking in successive rounds without stopping, the Shelley Grinder forces your brain to get to the core of your idea. There's no time for fluffy filler words and overthinking, just one fully crystallized idea in four minutes. You will find that you're actually more proficient with less time. Think of all the time you spend writing and rewriting your speeches, sorting out all the points you want to make. Parkinson's Law[38] says that when given more time to complete a project, you actually do less work and even find frivolous things to do to fill the time. In other words, the more time you have, the more you procrastinate.

Most people don't speak the way they write, so it is difficult to write a script for a speech and not sound like you're reading a white paper when you present it. In Chapter 5, I talked about how your experiences are best understood when spoken in everyday language. You'll find it even easier to speak more freely in your natural voice using the Shelley Grinder. When you reflect on an experience as you lived it, whether it's the moment you discovered a new product or acquired investors for a new business, you *know* the story. After talking about it in different ways with each sprint, you won't have to write it down word for word. This is how you reduce the anxiety of writing a script or having to memorize one.

Sprints help you articulate your thoughts as clear succinct ideas.

Sprints help you hone your focus on what is most important and eliminate extraneous details.

Sprints help you effectualize your decision-making process and reduce procrastination while structuring a speech.

Here's an example where the Shelley Grinder worked well for "Finn," a client I was coaching for an interview. The CEO conducting the interview was known for his rapid-fire style questioning. Feeling anxious, Finn wanted to show the CEO that he had the characteristics necessary for the position but also not bore him to death with long-winded answers. The Shelley Grinder was exactly how Finn achieved calm, clarity, and confidence for his interview. He later described the interview as, "Very friendly, very social, and conversational. I kept my cool throughout ... thanks [to] the terrific sessions of prep."

Your time is valuable, and with the Shelley Grinder, you'll make big improvements in your speaking skills without detracting from your busy life. You'll have the chance to experience it for yourself when you prepare for your next speaking event later in this chapter. But, for now, I have a few insights you'll want to know beforehand. Keep reading to find out what these are.

Leave the Features and Benefits on the Label

Features are the technical attributes of a product; benefits explain the product's value. Both are important but make for a dull read on any package or website. And simply reciting features and benefits will make your speech dull just the same.

Compare these two advertisements:

—*Amazing Mugs are Amazing! Our mugs are made with temperature-hardened, thermally robust high-carbon, double-walled for pyro resistant and cryogenic-compatible insulation technology, with micro polished, machine-washable chromium-nickel-based composite.*

—*Better Mugs are Best! Leslie had lost count of how many times he had nuked his lukewarm coffee by the time he got to the office each morning. One morning, he was digging around in the cabinet for his well-worn travel mug. Not able to find it, a mug called the Better Mug fell out of the cabinet with a hard bang onto the floor. Not a dent in the steel, he filled the mug with coffee and drove to work. For the next two hours, Leslie enjoyed a piping-hot cup in a shiny-dent free mug, completely unfazed by the fact that he was delayed in traffic the entire time!*

Which mug would you buy?

Mary Wells Lawrence was a trailblazing advertising industry legend in the 1970s. What set Lawrence apart from other executives was her ability to connect with people through humor and heart.

"Love is the keyword. Too many ads are cold, too filled with jargon. You have to talk person to person, with people, use people words and people terms," she said.

Her "I ♥ NY" campaign[39] did not sell tourism. The ads did not talk about the Michelin-star restaurants, the number of world-class theaters, or the internationally-famous museums New York had to offer. They told the story about the New York experience, something people cared about, in a language they could understand.

People buy things, follow brands, and subscribe to social channels because they are moved by a great experience. If all you do is share one mic-drop moment with your audience, you will move more people than if you rattled off a list of features and benefits.

> I always thought we were selling dreams, not clothes.
>
> —Irving Penn

You might think that it's not appropriate to speak about personal experiences in a professional environment. To that I say that my clients who use the Framework close deals and land more new jobs than those who don't. They facilitate meetings and workshops that are well-received and appreciated. They have taken on roles as thought leaders and elevated their relationships. Some have even used the Framework to develop their brand messaging and marketing campaigns.

You're reading this book because you want to become an excellent speaker, so now is not the time to fall back into your old ways of thinking. Doing more of the old way is not going to bring about new skills or improvements. I have coached over one thousand individuals of innumerable job positions and titles from wide-ranging industries to articulate their expertise time and again using real-life experiences—not theory.

You are your brand. If you want to be an articulate, compelling speaker, tell your story. It says so much more about you than the labels on your profile page.

What's Your Big Idea?

As clear as you are about your vision for your company, you have to be equally as clear with your big idea for any speaking event. The details are important, but if you are not one hundred percent clear about your one big idea, your audience will be confused about your message.

Using the tools of the Framework, you're now going to develop an actual, real-life talk that you have coming up on your schedule. Because the Remarkable Framework is universal, you can use it for any upcoming meeting, important call, product pitch, or reworking of an earlier presentation. Maybe your talk is a video series or facilitation you've been asked to lead. Choose one to explore using the Framework.

You're not going to structure your talk just yet. First you need to crystallize your big idea using the Shelley Grinder so all your stories and experiences have a solid foundation from which to branch. Everything you say in your talk is interconnected to your big idea, and like the Evergreen, must have a firmly-rooted trunk to balance its branches.

I use the Shelley Grinder for every talk I'm contracted to do, from workshops and keynotes to creating content for my YouTube channel. I warm up with the Power Up drill, then I do the Shelley Grinder, which you're about to do here.

After you have crystallized your big idea, you'll write it and the other elements of your talk on the Tree Grid. Taking a cue from my marketing consultancy, Big Idea, the Tree Grid is based on the Brand Message Matrix I created for clients to explore the elements of their brand. It was effective in helping them articulate their brand statement at a glance, which is why I am certain that it will help you develop a fluent speech.

Have a timer handy and open the Tree Grid section in your workbook by scanning the QR code or go to remarkableframework.com. Following is an example of the Tree Grid worksheet. Start with **Section A**.

<table>
<tr><th colspan="2">TREE GRID WORKSHEET</th></tr>
<tr><td colspan="2">Section D
My Call to Action
What action do you want your audience to take for your big idea?</td></tr>
<tr><td colspan="2"></td></tr>
<tr><td>Section B
What Is My Supporting Content?
What moments, experiences, examples, anecdotes, data, case studies, industry news, and so on best explain your big idea in Section A?</td><td>Section C
Why Am I Sharing This Content?
For each piece of content listed in Section B, write why it is important for you to share. What lesson have you learned or what value does this have for your audience?</td></tr>
<tr><td>1B</td><td>1C</td></tr>
<tr><td>2B</td><td>2C</td></tr>
<tr><td>3B</td><td>3C</td></tr>
<tr><td colspan="2">Section A
My Big Idea
What do you want your audience to know?</td></tr>
<tr><td colspan="2"></td></tr>
</table>

When doing the drill, don't worry about structuring the perfect statement, just allow your mind to freely explore wherever it wants to go, and make each sprint unique. The Shelley Grinder adds pressure while you speak. Pressure is good because with each timed sprint, more thoughts will emerge. I've included videos on this drill in the Shelley Grinder section of the workbook and on the Remarkable Framework playlist at youtube.com/@remarkablespeaking.

Whatever mistakes or fumbling that might happen, don't stop talking! Keep going with the timer; you might even surprise yourself at how quickly you can arrive at one very crystal clear answer.

SPRINT 1) Set the timer for ninety seconds and talk about your big idea. What do you want your audience to know?

SPRINT 2) Set the timer for sixty seconds and grind your idea with more clarity; let new thoughts emerge.

SPRINT 3) Set the timer for thirty seconds and continue to grind your idea even more.

Were you able to crystallize your big idea from a ninety-second sprint into thirty seconds? If you are not yet clear on your big idea or feel you need to refine it a little more, repeat Sprints 1 through 3 of the drill and take note of the following pro tips.

PRO TIP: You're not memorizing a phrase, you're exploring different ways to express your big idea with each sprint.

PRO TIP: Do not use crafty taglines or industry jargon. Speak in "I," "me," or "my" language to access a real moment and talk like your natural self.

PRO TIP: Take a breath.

For the fourth and final sprint in this drill, you want to repeat your big idea *and* end with your purpose to give context.

SPRINT 4) Set a timer for another sixty seconds and repeat your big idea—only this time use the full sixty seconds to speak in a relaxed and natural way, and end with your purpose. To do that, use one of the speaking prompts from the workbook; for example:

- I believe …
- My purpose in sharing this …
- Why I feel strongly about ...
- My goal for our discussion …

Once you can articulate your big idea, write it in **Section A** of the Tree Grid worksheet.

You can record yourself doing the entire four-minute drill, one sprint after the other, but don't watch any of them until you've completed all four. When you have completed all four sprints, watch the recording. What did you notice about your speaking from the first sprint to the fourth?

When your big idea can stand on its own in sixty seconds, you will be able to speak about it for ten minutes or two hours with greater focus, comfort, and confidence.

Next, you'll connect the branches to the trunk by filling out **Sections B** and **C** on the Tree Grid.

Sprint to the Finish Line

How do you come up with content? How do you know what to say? How do you decide what content in your story bank is the best to use for your talk and what should be eliminated?

Let me answer all that by starting with how to come up with content. Your story bank is a collection of your content; i.e., any of these interchangeable stories that support your big idea: moments, experiences, examples, anecdotes, data, case studies, industry news, and so on. You want to talk about what you know because a story does a lot of explaining.

Your content doesn't have to be something you have personally experienced. Maybe it's something you heard about from a competitor or read in the trades. It could be the moment that you arrived at the data or something that you experienced as far back as college or grade school. You might remember a teacher or mentor who influenced how you do business today. Now that's something worth talking about!

If you need to protect the privacy of individuals or companies and proprietary information, you don't have to mention names. You can replace "Alphabet and Google's CEO Sundar Pichai" with "The CEO of an internet tech company." Specific moments doesn't mean specific names.

Section A of the Tree Grid worksheet now has your big idea written in it. In **Section B**, you're going to sprint and write a list of one to three stories that best explain your idea. You may have more, and that's good; allow your mind to wander. As you rediscover more moments, you can add them to **Section B** of the worksheet. You may have a few from Chapter 5's story bank that will work for this talk. If so, add them here.

You don't have to go into detail or worry about which ones to use at this step. For now, you are just making a list using a brief descriptor as a speaking prompt.

Okay, let's sprint! Set a timer for sixty seconds and start writing your list in **Section B**.

All finished?

Now for each moment in **Section B**, you're going to write why it's important for you to share in **Section C**. What lesson have you learned from each moment? What value does each experience have for your audience? Think about each story as a branch on the tree; you're connecting each branch to the tree trunk that is your big idea.

So set a timer for sixty seconds and write your list in **Section C**.

At this stage, your Tree Grid worksheet is filling up with the elements of your speech: your big idea and all your supporting content. But you're not out of the woods quite yet! You're going to use the Shelley Grinder to figure out what to say. Choose one moment from **Section B** of the Tree Grid and why that piece of content is important for you to share from its counterpart in **Section C**.

> **SPRINT 1)** Set the timer for ninety seconds and talk about a moment from **Section B** and why it's important to share from **Section C**.
>
> **SPRINT 2)** Set the timer for sixty seconds and grind the same moment, allowing new perspectives to emerge.
>
> **SPRINT 3)** Set the timer for thirty seconds and continue to grind that moment once again.
>
> **SPRINT 4)** Set a timer for another sixty seconds and repeat, ending with one of the speaking prompts:
>
> - It's important for me to tell you …
> - An interesting lesson that I learned …
> - The valuable takeaway is …
> - I think you'll appreciate this …

Were you able to speak your ninety-second sprint and grind it into thirty seconds? Were you able to bring it all together in Sprint 4 in sixty seconds?

> **PRO TIP:** If you default to reciting features and benefits jargon, use the speaking prompts in your workbook to reflect on a moment. To connect with people, you want to use people words and people terms.

> **PRO TIP:** To talk about a specific moment, use a speaking prompt with "I," "me," or "my" language to help you focus on what it is you want to say.

> **PRO TIP:** If you're rambling, just stop. Breathe. Make space, and repeat your big idea. You'll come back much stronger and more confident.

Remember, the Shelley Grinder is a speaking drill, so the goal is to keep your speaking natural and free from memorization. For an example of how this is done, listen to the podcast where I coached the host live on his show using the Shelley Grinder. You can find the audio hyperlink to the full episode, "An Exercise That Will Make You Memorable," in the Shelley Grinder section of your workbook and on the Remarkable Framework playlist at youtube.com/@remarkablespeaking.

You made it through the Shelley Grinder, congratulations! You've just completed your first talking point. Repeat this drill for all of your content from **Sections B** and **C**.

Now, having talked about your big idea and supporting stories, what do you want people to do? Ask them with a call to action. You may not be selling anything for purchase per se, but you are sharing information. Your call to action is an opportunity to connect with people and nurture future relationships. It is like the crown of the evergreen that nurtures the life of the tree. There's more to read about nurturing audiences coming up in Chapter 9, so hold that thought. For now, get ready for another sprint.

SPRINT 1) Set the timer for ninety seconds and talk about what action you want your audience to take for your big idea. Here are some prompts to guide you:

- Here's what I believe we can do …
- This is what I'm suggesting …
- I invite you to …
- Many of my clients have had success with …

SPRINT 2) Set the timer for sixty seconds and grind for a second time, allowing new strategies to emerge.

SPRINT 3) Set the timer for thirty seconds and continue to grind that action once again.

SPRINT 4) Set a timer for another sixty seconds and repeat.

When you can successfully convey your call to action, go to your Tree Grid worksheet and write it in **Section D**.

For every second that you're doing the drills, you're refining your content and beginning to see the forest for the trees. Do you feel a difference in how you're connecting to your key messages when speaking about them? Can you talk about your big idea in a conversational and spontaneous way?

When you're crystal clear that you can articulate the elements you've collected in your Tree Grid, you're ready to use the Evergreen tool to organize the structure of your speech. Plant a tree and nurture it to grow, and you won't leave your audience hanging on a limb.

That's a Wrap

The trunk is now firmly rooted and balanced with its branches, so it's time to bring the canopy into full view. You've got your big idea, your supporting content, and your call to action, and you know how to say it. Here's where you'll use the Evergreen worksheet to organize the elements of the Tree Grid to strengthen the effectiveness of your big idea.

Turn to the Evergreen worksheet in your workbook.

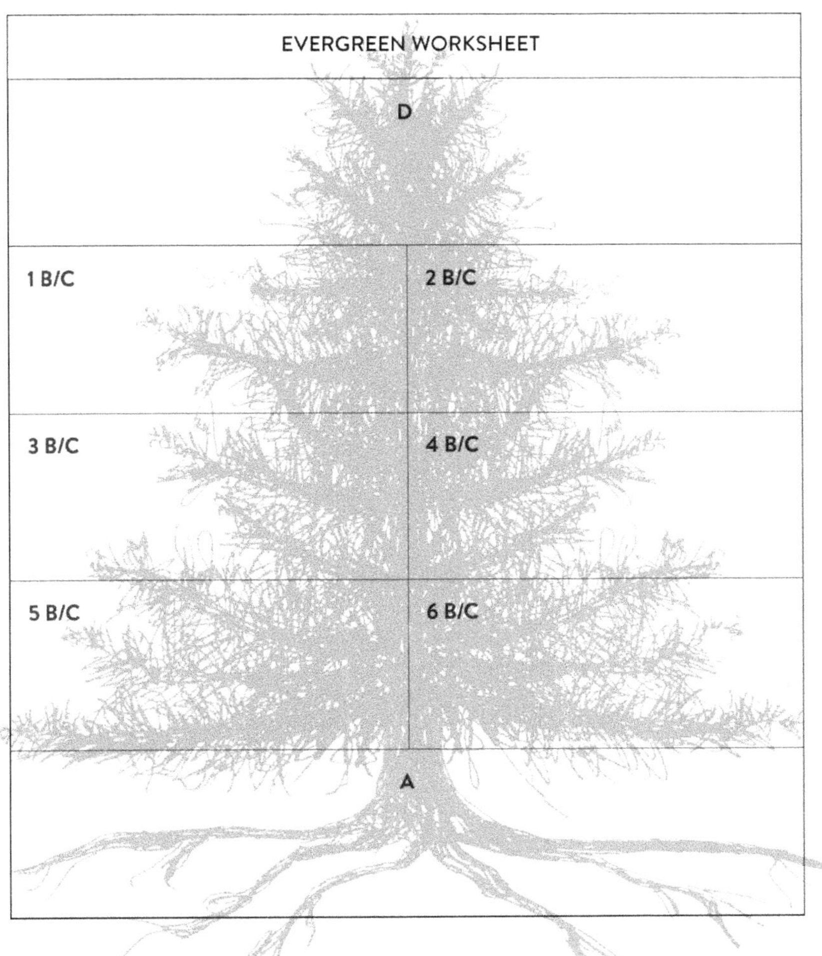

Looking at the Evergreen worksheet, you'll notice that **Sections A, B/C**, and **D** correlate with the sections on the Tree Grid. Go ahead and write your big idea and call to action in **Sections A** and **D** on the Evergreen worksheet. Now you have a visual for how to organize your content, the branches, to support your big idea, the trunk, from the root to the crown.

Write each story on a small Post-it® and add them to the **B/C Sections** of the Evergreen. The bottom of the tree is the beginning of your speech and, filling in content working your way to the top, your call to action is the wrap up.

As you add and move your content around the Evergreen, be sure all your moments, experiences, examples, anecdotes, data, case studies, or industry news reinforce your big idea. If the content doesn't reinforce what it is you want to say, archive it in your story bank for another talk. *Always bring the conversation back to your big idea.*

People need to hear your message more than once for it to click. This is really valuable when you're presenting complex subjects and bigger scale ideas. Your audience will resonate with your big idea when they can see a bird's-eye view of the canopy, not just a branch or pine needle!

> **PRO TIP:** Throughout your talk, repeat your big idea a lot and often. Following the advice of Aristotle, the master of rhetoric, "Tell them what you're going to tell them. Tell them. Tell them what you told them."

> **PRO TIP:** If you have so many Post-its® on the Evergreen that you can no longer see the tree, that's a sign that you probably have too much content.

> **PRO TIP:** Wrap things up, and say your call to action with conviction. A weak ending would be like a sentence without a period.

The Framework rescued me from a potential disaster. I was invited to give a presentation on self-promotion for the leadership team of a humanitarian nonprofit. But for some reason, my calendar said I was scheduled to do a podcast talking about leadership and executive presence. I showed up on Zoom that morning and quickly realized my mistake, and within fifteen minutes of logging on, I had tapped into my story bank and reorganized one of the fastest Evergreen structures I have ever done. I quickly jotted down what I wanted them to know about self-promotion, including three stories and two interactive elements to support my big idea. I even had an extra minute to open an old slide deck and edit the slides. Boom! Just like that, I had a forty-five-minute presentation with slides completed in under five minutes! The flexibility of the Framework turned a potential disaster into a remarkable success. One attendee commented: "I initially thought the workshop would be another set of generic tips on becoming a better public speaker, but it turned out to be so much more … I wanted to write to express how inspired I felt by the session."

Crystallize your big idea in four minutes, and you won't have to worry about what to say for the next forty minutes. Reinforce how you got to your big idea by updating your key takeaways in Chapter 10 on page 181.

Now you have a structure for your speech and the skills for how to talk about it. You don't need more planning than that. The Remarkable Framework is your plan.

In Chapters 8 and 9, I'll show you how to apply the Framework and put it into action like determining the timeliness of speeches and other presentation tips. Which brings me to a question I am asked by clients: "What strategies help with memorization for a speech?" What I share next might surprise you.

CHAPTER 8
BE THE BRIDGE, NOT THE BARRIER

The Memorization Trap

I am so bad at memorizing. It is guaranteed that as soon as I try to memorize a talk, I'll forget a quote or even an entire part of a speech. I don't know how other people do it, but, for me, having to commit facts, statistics, or exact quotes to memory is a sure way to ensure that I will fail to recall them when I need to.

Maybe that's the case for you too. You feel a twitch of anxiety coming on, the words are on the tip of your tongue, and then they're gone. You have forgotten what you want to say. Memorizing adds pressure to an already tense situation.

Memories are formed by strengthening connections between neurons in the brain. Pressure can interfere with the connection process by flooding the brain with hormones like cortisol that make it harder to focus and store information effectively. That added pressure of memorization essentially causes a temporary traffic jam in your brain.

So how can you be exact and remember what you want to say if you find memorization difficult?

You write it down. An analysis of several studies on memory concluded that physically writing something out by hand increases your ability to remember it.[40] Similar to building a habit through repetition, your hand-brain connection through writing activates your neural pathways.

A separate study highlights evidence that, compared to typing, handwriting boosts communication between brain regions linked to memory.[41] This argues that the slower, more deliberate process of writing allows the brain to absorb and retain information more effectively.

Here's where the writing sprint becomes even more valuable. Writing down brief descriptors for your content in the Tree Grid and Story Bank worksheets not only helps you document your talking points for your presentation, it also reinforces your memory of them. Additionally, writing notecards to use during your presentation further strengthens your memory.

Notating your research is a good thing as long as, whatever form you're using—notecards, teleprompters, cue cards, or mnemonics like acronyms or rhymes—you're not writing out or reading an entire script word for word.

When I prepare for my speaking engagements, I no longer write a script. Instead, I use the Evergreen worksheet and write my talking points on notecards. The process gives me confidence that I won't forget key points, but I also won't be desperately fumbling to remember all the facts during my talk.

The first time I ditched my script—and I'm not going to lie here—I was terrified of having to present with only a few notecards in hand. Ironically, I was about to give a seminar on confidence to graduate students at a west coast university. But the strangest thing happened. I put my notecards on the podium, and when I gave my talk, I never once looked at them. The Q&A that followed confirmed that I covered all my talking points by the type of questions the students were asking.

Doing the Framework's writing and speaking drills in preparation for my talk had strengthened the neural pathways in my brain to store the content. It was much easier and so much less pressure to present without relying on a script.

> **PRO TIP:** Write a quote or statistic from your Evergreen worksheet on a notecard or create a slide with a few bullet points in your presentation deck. The cards and slides function as cues to help guide you through your talk.

My turning point—where I could comfortably speak spontaneously and ditch a script completely—was when I recorded a promo video for a webinar that I was asked to present. The topic was how to answer questions for a job interview to make an impact. I wanted to have the exact words to express my thoughts and feelings and wrote a lengthy script highlighting key phrases.

I lost count of the number of takes I recorded for a thirty-second video. When I looked at my watch, an hour had passed. I got so hung up on saying the right words that the task was excruciating and became the reason why I hated recording videos.

I tore up my script and said, "Shelley, you've got thirty seconds and one take." I hit record, and, without hesitation, I got right to the point with a moment when I got laid off and posted the video. It was one of the top-ranked posts for engagement I had done at that time. There was an uptick in registration and an outpouring of support. "Shelley, I can so relate, I was laid off too!" and "Thank you for posting!"

One take. If I took to heart the Framework and used the One-Take Video Message drill, I would have saved myself take after take after take.

> If you tell the truth,
> you don't have to remember anything.
>
> —Mark Twain

You might default to the idea that speaking in a professional environment is full of restrictions. I'm not sure who came up with those rules, but you can be professional and bring humanness into your talk.

I don't have a character for different speeches. There's one of me, and there's one of you. When you're presenting something that is meaningful to you, you want to be conversational and speak in your natural voice. Like you learned in Chapter 3, feeling emotions is not a bad thing because if you want to amaze audiences, you need to let them know how amazed you are.

Over-rehearsing to memorize a script can make you more nervous than you already are. It takes up valuable time, and you risk disconnecting from your words and your audience. So don't fall into the trap of memorizing. When you let go of the script and talk about what you know, you'll discover the words you say will reveal your mic-drop moment.

If people are coming to hear you talk, they will be very disappointed if instead they have to watch you read. Put down the script; I'm about to give you more ideas on how to not put audiences into a coma.

Don't Put Your Audience Into a Data Coma

There will be times when your client demands that you report the data. You may try to cram a ton of facts into your presentation, but it will be the client who then has to memorize the facts in order to understand what you're saying. So the real challenge is how to communicate complex, necessary information without your audience suffering from cognitive overload.

The solution: Talk about the human side of the facts using stories. It's not the data that's the problem per se, but, rather, the way it's presented. Reciting data and facts is not usually what moves people, so you have to find a way to present those without compromising on the emotion. None of the data means anything until a human experiences it.

> Maybe stories are just data with a soul.
>
> —Brené Brown

When building a bridge of communication, it is more efficient to deliver a single, crystal clear message than several muddy messages. If the eighty-twenty Pareto Principle[42] holds true, then eighty percent of your presentation results from twenty percent of what you say. This means that if you want to get your message across really well, telling a story *is* the twenty percent.

A story is a comprehensive way to illustrate the complexity of the subject no matter who's in the audience. A story doesn't oversimplify your talk for experts; instead, experts perceive it as confirmation that you know what you're talking about. And a story doesn't overcomplicate your talk for lay people; instead, they will be able to understand your point and use it as an opportunity to learn.

In writing his book *Hidden Potential*,[43] Adam Grant confessed, "The book made me more comfortable using my own stories. I was accused of using data as a crutch. I shied away from personal stories because it felt self-centered and idiosyncratic. If there's something I've learned from something I've lived, why would I not share it?"

No matter how technical or nontechnical your talk is, you're still sharing information, so you want to make sure you capture your audience's attention right from the start.

If they snooze, you lose.

At just eight seconds, some claim the human ability to pay attention rivals that of a goldfish. However, that myth has been widely debunked by neuropsychologists and scientists who have actually studied goldfish as a model for memory formation and learning.[44]

In her research on learning, PhD and author Patti Shank notes, "There is no set attention span … But there is a need to gain and keep attention because there are internal and external things competing for attention all the time."[45] Shank explains that attention and memory are related. "We are processing information from outside (for example, what someone is saying and images we see) using working memory and linking what we are processing to information from the inside (thoughts, feelings, and what we already know)."[46] In other words, the brain is attentive when it's stimulated, like hearing a story, and it clicks. That's attention grabbing, even at eight seconds!

But the data! They want the data!

Data is important, but there's a time and place to bring it into your presentation. Once you have grabbed your audience's attention with a story, you then can cite the data to substantiate your point. If people are interested and want to know more, you can offer to follow up with a fact sheet or white paper. When you have a captive audience, that's when a deep dive into the facts is more engaging.

If and when you do have to mention specific facts, whether you're the person giving the debrief or a subject-matter expert, I suggest using notecards to recite them as they are written. It's imperative to get the facts right when there's an opportunity to do so because accuracy builds trust and understanding.

When presenting complex information, you want to meet your audience where they are and make sure they understand. There's often an expectation that everyone in the room should know all the acronyms and technical terms, but rarely does anyone raise the issue when they don't because they feel shamed, possibly believing that they're supposed to know.

I can't tell you how many times I've been in meetings where someone drops acronyms that I have not heard of before or have a different meaning in another industry. If that person had explained the acronym with a story, then I wouldn't be Googling random letters discreetly on my phone to keep up with the conversation.

> **PRO TIP:** Whether it's data, acronyms, or a direct quote that you're using in your presentation, give your audience some space to take it all in, and check to see if they understand. Ask, "Are you with me?" or "Did I explain that well?" Here's where you can talk about another example from your story bank. "Let me explain it this way" or "This is what I did for another client."

Sharing your stories helps to limit confusion when you're presenting data and facts that can be overwhelming, making your talk accessible to everyone. It's like meeting a new associate: You've heard their name mentioned in conversation, but when you finally meet them face-to-face, you're "putting a name to a face." You want your presentations to be the bridge to your big idea, not the barrier.

The Ebbinghaus Forgetting Curve[47] suggests most people forget fifty percent of new information within an hour of hearing it and continue forgetting upward of seventy percent in the following twenty-four hours. Use your time wisely, and keep your talk simple and to the point.

But "less is more" doesn't stop at your speech itself. Keep reading to learn how to craft slides that amplify what you're talking about, not replace what you're saying.

The Paradox of Plenty

I remember sitting through a one-hour webinar where the speaker talked us through 101 slides. I kid you not. Taking into account the introduction and the Q&A, the speaker had approximately 0.445 seconds to talk about each slide. He was talking so fast, he was tripping over his tongue. If you were to ask me what I took away from that PowerPoint death march: One picture is worth a thousand words.

One powerful image can spark your brain to connect to a single memory without using a thousand words.

A scientific study on multitasking found that the human brain cannot effectively perform several tasks simultaneously.[48] It is true that you can do more than one task at a time; however, your brain lowers its capacity to function when it's trying to process all the stimuli. According to the study, the human brain has evolved to focus on a single task. At best, it can only process a small part of any one task at any one time. When switching back and forth between multiple tasks, you're prone to make errors and fatigue easily because you're expending energy just to focus.

As a speaker, your job is to create a great experience for your audience. You don't want them to work hard in order to understand what you're saying. Their brains won't remember fifty percent of what you've said within an hour of hearing all the details, so save your words—and their attention—and simplify with an image.

> The ability to simplify means to eliminate the unnecessary so that the necessary may speak.
>
> —Hans Hofmann

Think of a children's picture book. Typically, you'll find lots of colorful drawings and a few words. Simplifying is not diminishing the integrity of what you're presenting; it's making it easier to digest.

Whether your big idea is complex or moderately straightforward, you want to be efficient in how you present it. Creating fewer slides with strong imagery and fewer words will allow your audience members to better comprehend what you're saying because they're not struggling to read and listen simultaneously, or worse, disengaging due to mental overload altogether.

One of my signature talks is a ninety-minute presentation with twelve slides. This talk on confidence includes an introduction, a few interactive elements, and a Q&A. One of my clients had this to say about my talk: "We had a powerful session investing in our own professional and personal development. A huge 'Thank you!' to Shelley Goldstein, facilitator, magician, and powerful leader for guiding us through the data and how to overcome these [obstacles] successfully."

With twelve slides for a ninety-minute presentation, I did not have a slide for every talking point. The slides I did include had either one captivating image, statistic, or a quote. For my slides with text, I kept each one concise with no more than three bullet points. Instead of multitasking, my audience was able to track what I was saying and not miss vital information. Follow the eighty-twenty rule and save a lot of time with fewer words and fewer slides.

The Evergreen can help you decide where the appropriate place is to insert your slides in your presentation. Slides are the visual aid for the content that you listed in **Section B/C** of the Tree Grid worksheet. Write a descriptor for the slide on a Post-it® and add it to the Evergreen worksheet. Make sure the slide is connected to your big idea and that you can clearly state why it's important for you to share.

> **PRO TIP:** If you have a twenty-five-minute presentation, a good slide count is six. You'll want to keep the length of your speaking time per slide between one and three minutes, but not more than three minutes. Doesn't sound like enough time? Remember, with the Shelley Grinder, you crystallized your big idea into thirty seconds. Three minutes will feel like an eternity!

> **PRO TIP:** If you've been given sixty minutes to give your talk, structure it for fifty minutes. The extra ten minutes will give you the confidence that you've covered all your talking points. You'll be more relaxed because you're not racing the clock, and you'll have space to engage in Q&A. If there are not a lot of questions for the Q&A, introduce a new story or revisit the facts and elaborate on the details.

> **PRO TIP:** Go to remarkableframework.com to see my resource on building out a presentation, The Slide Deck Blueprint: Must-Dos for Every Presenter.

In workshops that are scheduled for two or more hours or full-day immersions, it can be challenging for attendees to stay attentive even with slides. Engage them with interactive elements, and time them throughout the workshop, adding more value.

You can try activities like handouts for I AM writing drills. Run some live polling where people raise their hands, and then you can talk about the results in real time. You can also direct attendees into small breakout discussions or speed networking groups.

I coached "Sabine," a client who was speaking at an international environmental conference in Paris. She planned to show three three-minute videos during a twenty-minute presentation. I encouraged her to reduce the number of videos to two and introduce a five-minute interactive element in the middle of her speech. The stage was huge, and there were over two hundred people in attendance. When she asked the audience to stand up and participate during the presentation, just like that, people formed into small groups and interacted. Her Instagram was flooded with praise about the amazing experience long after the conference ended.

If you choose to work with videos or props in your presentation, I strongly recommend that you do a lot of run-throughs while incorporating the visual aids. Consider creating a backup checklist and include things like having a physical copy of your speech outline, extra props, a power cord, and a duplicate drive with your presentation. Arrive at the venue early to secure internet connection and logistics. This is one of the rare exceptions where a lot of rehearsing and having backups is vital because minor word flubs can go unnoticed, but bigger technical difficulties can be a disaster.

With the Evergreen, you have lots of flexibility to adjust to any timeframe and choose only the most essential elements to include when creating the structure for your presentation. A well-defined presentation is the vehicle that brings your vision to life and your audience into the conversation.

Stop Apologizing!

There are legitimate reasons to be apologetic for some things, but when it comes to looking at your notes or forgetting a word or dealing with an external distraction like an interruption during your talk, there's no need to apologize.

A good part of the planet's population has experienced Zoom at least once since 2020. Cameras freeze, wifi signals drop off, and what about that mute/unmute button that people still can't find? These things happen all the time. If you didn't hurt anyone, what are you apologizing for?

I was contracted to develop new partnership strategies for a prop house that serviced Hollywood's filmmaking studios. The prop company was located about five miles from a brand-new, state-of-the-art studio. I got buy-in from the studio owner on a partnership as their exclusive prop house.

Later that week at the prop house, they called for a meeting with the CEO, president, VP of sales, and a few members from the board. I put together a presentation outlining the opportunity and asked to have it added to the agenda.

About five minutes into my presentation, the VP and one of the board members broke out into a side conversation. I stopped mid-sentence and apologized. The two continued talking, and another board member joined their conversation. I apologized again and waited. I finally got their attention, but, feeling the weight of my apology, I rushed to finish and did not fully present the opportunity.

Several days afterward, I found out another prop house had secured the deal with the studio. When I mentioned this to the CEO, he remembered my presentation but said he didn't see the significance because I appeared doubtful. Shame on the group for dismissing my presentation and losing out on a partnership. Shame on me for apologizing for something that I did not do and not speaking up for what I believed in.

Apologizing unnecessarily is a distraction, like the pink elephant in the room. Bringing attention to something, "Wait, wait, wait! Can I start again?" because someone interrupts you or you pull up the wrong slide undermines your credibility.

Don't apologize if you've been interrupted; interject and move the conversation forward.

Don't apologize and "BUT" your way to excuses and obstacles that don't exist. Take a deep breath, and reframe your self-talk.

Don't apologize for not having the perfect words. People don't remember every word you say; they remember how you made them feel in that moment when they heard you.

Don't apologize because you don't know the answer to something. Be honest that you don't know, and share something you do know.

Don't apologize for ending your presentation. End a few minutes before you think you need to, and make your last impression a strong one.

Your talk means a lot to you, and your audience is there to hear what you have to say. When you apologize unnecessarily, the pink elephant in the room gets a lot pinker and a lot bigger. Take a breath, and reframe what you think needs an apology to "Please excuse me" or "Bear with me for a moment."

Maybe you believe that more preparation will help you avoid errors or reduce anxiety. Keep reading to discover the downside of preparation.

Prepare to Unprepare

What if preparation is not the answer to a good presentation?

You can guarantee that in presentations, as in life, things will not go one hundred percent as planned. You can't anticipate what will happen with a Zoom connection or if the meeting will be delayed or whether there will be a last-minute change in the agenda. Preparation can bring a false sense of confidence and diminish your authenticity.

I was hired to facilitate a virtual workshop for the leadership and development team at one of the big credit card companies. As an outside vendor, the process of working with a large corporation involves a lot of pre-planning with its different departments and levels of management. The day of the sixty-minute workshop, I logged on fifteen minutes early for the sound check, but the meeting link wasn't working. I emailed the team and found out that the link that had been shared was from a past event. It was sixteen minutes past the hour before I received a new link. I could sense the panic of the hosts, and I now had less than forty minutes to lead fifty-five people as they slowly trickled into the virtual room. The workshop got underway, but I had to make drastic changes in real time. I have to say that I managed to keep my cool because, using the Framework, every story was interconnected with my big idea. No matter which stories I chose to eliminate due to time constraints, the integrity of the workshop remained intact.

A few days later, the copartner of the leadership and development team emailed me: "Shelley, your professionalism and enthusiasm for the topic and strong presence made this event a huge hit! We have gotten raving feedback, and I felt it was important to share on how you made a mark on our members! We are set up and ready for workshop number two!"

Prepare for the audience you expect, but listen to the audience before you.

—Shelley Goldstein

How many times have you been faced with a client crisis and thought, "I've never seen this before, but we'll figure it out" or "I'm up for the challenge, let's work on this together." None of those crises were a barrier that kept you from moving forward. It was your flexibility that led you to a solution and made it a great experience.

The Remarkable Framework gives you the flexibility to adapt your outline to any talk or presentation. When you are crystal clear about your big idea, your content, and your call to action, the trunk of the Evergreen is firmly rooted into the ground. You do not have to rewrite your entire speech; you simply move elements around because every branch balances your big idea. That's all the preparation you need.

First learn
to make, then
the higher skill,
learning to unmake.

Prepare to unprepare and break free from the agenda. Take a minute to add this chapter's key takeaways to the worksheet in Chapter 10 on page 181.

I thought it would be interesting to reach out to clients and business owners, as stakeholders, and ask for feedback about being on the receiving end of presentations. Among the common pitfalls they shared: Lost interest due to conventional introductions peppered with clichés and presenters who talked excessively without listening to their needs. The results are compiled in my speaking resource, Eliminate These Don'ts and Win Clients at remarkableframework.com.

Whether things fall apart or fall into place, there are ways that you can leverage your message and influence others. I'm not talking about being an influencer—that's short-term. In Chapter 9, I talk about long-term results: Building your legacy.

CHAPTER 9
LEVERAGE YOUR MESSAGE

From Monologue to Dialogue

You've probably been subjected to conversations talking about the weather or been to presentations that feel like boring monologues. If you didn't find it interesting on the receiving end, your audience probably wouldn't think so either. Think of the hours you've spent preparing a thirty-minute speech. Perhaps you dug so deep into the details that you completely lost focus of the first minute. But that very first minute is your primary opportunity to capture your audience's attention.

Madeleine Albright, former Secretary of State and UN Ambassador under the Clinton administration, had an extensive collection of brooches that she wore as a communication tool for cultural diplomacy.[49]

Following the first Persian Gulf War, Iraq was required to accept UN inspections. When Saddam Hussein, then-president of Iraq, refused to comply, the outspoken Albright criticized him. He called her "an unparalleled serpent," and from that moment forward, during any relations she had with Iraq, she wore her antique snake pin. Even without words, Albright was engaging in a dialogue, and her message undoubtedly got through to her intended listeners!

When Russia was caught tapping the State Department, she wore a giant bug pin. When sending messages of optimism and hope, Secretary Albright wore pins with balloons, butterflies, or flowers. When talks stalled with foreign nationals, she wore crab or turtle pins.

She once remarked, "You think that the heads of state only have serious conversations, but they actually often begin with the weather or, 'I really like your tie.'" But she broke through these formal, stiff introductions. Albright used her brooches to spark conversation at the highest levels of government. Her pins changed the way she influenced conversations and meetings by captivating her audiences and setting the tone, ensuring that she leveraged her message. You too have that opportunity in the first minute of your talk.

Don't squander it by defaulting to talking about the weather—the "safe" but not interesting or memorable conversation. Instead, like Albright, take that moment, that first minute of your speech, and leverage your message in a creative way with a story. At first, it may feel uncomfortable to start conversations with your team or board of directors or before a meeting or speech when no one else is making introductions in this way. It's something new. But, over time, you'll start to see how people take notice and click with what you're saying. With your story bank, you no longer have to rely on the weather for small talk, which can come across as trivial and inauthentic, unless, of course, the weather is relevant to the conversation!

When you capture your audience's attention, you avoid monologuing at them; instead, you've essentially engaged them in a dialogue. However you convey your message, the key is to be relatable. You're in the people business; you serve people, and you work with people. Don't provoke a boring talk with a boring introduction. Find common ground by sharing an analogy or comparison story.

For example, by starting your speech with a sport or hobby experience, people will be able to relate and often find common interests. Some may initially wonder what basketball has to do with the meeting. But, like Albright and her pins, at least you've got their attention! And they may even want to know more.

One of my clients, "Esme," was a doctor completing her residency. She needed coaching for the interviews required to become a board-certified physician. In our sessions, she told me that she had earned a scholarship playing state-level basketball in grade school. I asked her what made her so good on the court. She said she learned that if players were not receptive, they would miss seeing the ball when it's being passed to them. She explained that she had to be fast but calm to navigate the chaos on the court and get the ball into the basket.

I then asked if her skills on the court compared to her time working at the hospital. She realized that, yes, by focusing on the patient in the chaos of the emergency room, she kept her calm and knew exactly how to treat them as well as delegate procedures to the team. Her leadership, problem solving, and teamwork skills there were very much mirrored playing basketball.

Playing a sport at state level or navigating a hospital emergency room involves high stakes and high pressure. Do you see the analogy? In addition to detailing her tasks at the hospital, Esme was able to describe her soft skills by telling a relatable story about playing team sports. Illustrating transferable skills through stories highlights why you are so good at what you do and reveals your bigger purpose. It's not only what you've learned in your current role that matters, it's what you've learned in every role over the course of your life.

I have a resource called Unlocking Presentation Excellence: Insights from Elite Athletes. In it, you'll learn how to elevate your presentations by tapping into the pre-game strategies of peak-performing athletes. Find it at remarkableframework.com.

Like the doctor, you can leverage your transferable skills to substantiate the diagnostics. You can show compassion and still come across as professional, practical, and technical. When thinking about everything you've experienced in your life, keep leveraging the question: "Where else can I transfer my skills?"

I was at a friend's wedding, laughing with the people sitting at my table. I've known the bride for years but had only met the groom a few times. Out of nowhere, I hear my name being called. "Our first toast is from Shelley Goldstein." The announcement caught me completely off guard. As I walked up to the microphone, I thought, "Is this a mistake?" I had nothing prepared. I got to the mic and looked around the room. As the first speaker, I had their full attention. That is when my adrenaline spiked. *Holy crap, what am I going to say?* I blurted out, "Do you have the right Shelley Goldstein?" People laughed. After a pause, I then said, "Well, maybe the happy couple invited me to kick things off because by profession, I'm a keynote speaker." There was more laughter, and I paused again. I did not intend for my jokes to be a shameless plug; I took those moments to breathe. As my nerves began to settle, I started to tell the story of how I had met the groom.

I had reached out to him, a seasoned lawyer, about an opportunity I was up for at a local law firm. It turned out that he knew one of the partners at the firm and made the introduction. It was rather bold because, at that point, I hadn't met the groom in person. Although the project didn't pan out, I was glad to see that the groom did! People started clapping and cheering as I walked back to my table. One guest actually yelled out, "I loved the pauses!"

Speaking remarkably is about having authentic, remarkable conversations. Leveraging a conversation with interesting dialogue for a seminar, lunch and learn, or even a friend's wedding is more than simply talking people through an agenda. That would be like citing the table of contents to explain your favorite part of a book.

When people align with you, laugh with you, and cry with you, you've got their attention. You can transition from what could be a boring monologue to an intriguing dialogue; it's all in how you present the information.

Pull the Break on Your Elevator Pitch

Otis is the name you've probably seen on most elevators you've been on. Elisha Graves Otis not only invented the first safety passenger elevator, his story originated the term "elevator pitch."[50]

Elevators existed long before Otis, but people did not feel safe riding them because the retaining ropes would break, sending the lift plummeting to the ground floor. In 1854, Otis premiered his elevator safety-brake system at P.T. Barnum's Traveling World's Fair in New York.

Otis built a three-storey elevator shaft that had no walls so the crowds could see the elevator frame dangling by its problematic ropes. In a live demonstration, Otis rode his elevator to the top floor and then cut the ropes with a saber. The crowds let out terrifying screams as the elevator went into free fall until Otis launched his safety-brake system that stopped the elevator and prevented him from plummeting to his death.

That demonstration changed the perception of elevators, and with the help of P.T. Barnum, one of the greatest marketers of his time, the elevator pitch was coined. The success of elevators wasn't a sales pitch pushing features and benefits, it was an experience that scared people into a moment they'll never forget.

You don't have to construct an elevator shaft to deconstruct your pitch. Persuasive selling is about sharing an experience that excites you and excites your prospects into wanting what you've got. Invite them to continue the conversation with a call back, an opportune time to share the fact sheet and take a deeper dive into the data.

By now, you know that I am a fan of networking. Networking is great for many things, including, as I discussed in Chapter 4, an attainable way to practice speaking and initiate conversations. I remember one particular networking group I was a part of. In the breakout room, as expected, one by one, people jumped into pitch mode with their allotted one minute. One guy rattled off a barrage of facts and features so quickly, it was difficult to keep up with his speed-talk.

Not able to comprehend much of what he said, I had no interest in pursuing any further conversation with him. It was only months later, after I went through the grueling process of hiring a marketing service, that I was paired up in the same breakout room with the same fact-and-features guy. It was then that I learned that he ran a marketing agency. He shared some really interesting stories about his business that day. Unfortunately for both of us, it was a missed opportunity.

Refer to the Framework whenever you need to, and sprint to explore new experiences and perspectives about an idea that you have to talk about. You'll keep the dialogue fresh and interesting for you and your prospects. This is even more important with the expansion of virtual and in-person events. We default to the name-title-tagline boilerplate because that's the way it's been done for so long, but it's not the only way it can be done.

Nobody wants to be sold, but you are interested in things that will improve your life—things that you need and that you'll use, or special things you want to reward yourself with.

Everyone is selling something. Products and services, talents when interviewing for a job, reasoning for making decisions, and ideas during collaboration. Even on a personal level, you're selling your opinions about sports and hobbies or restaurants you've experienced. In all those situations, you can un-pitch and have real conversations that convert. Your prospects will be more likely to connect with you and your product or service to reap their own benefits.

Whether they're ready to buy or not, it's not the end of a transaction. This is the beginning of a relationship. That's when you get their permission for the call back. Dial into the next subchapter to learn ways to continue delivering more value.

Get the Call Back

As a speaker, it is to your advantage to approach any kind of speech, un-pitch, or facilitation from the point of view that you're sharing information. It's not from the assumption that everyone is broken and you can fix them; rather, you're inviting people into a conversation and creating space for connection and exchange. It's the spirit of reciprocity.

There is a well-known study on reciprocity where restaurant servers who gave customers a handful of mints along with their checks got bigger tips than servers who did not.[51] The researchers concluded that when you give or offer something to people, the natural tendency is for them to feel a measure of indebtedness to you.

There are a lot of chances for reciprocity when you're speaking. One is leveraging your call to action that I mentioned in Chapter 7. I believe every talk should include a call to action as the golden opportunity to stay connected and build relationships with your audience. Whether you want them to make a purchase, sign up for a newsletter, or just learn something new, offer them a mint.

Here are some call to action examples (also available in the Speaking Prompts section of the workbook for reference) to wrap up your next talk:

- May I email you the fact sheet (or white paper) with more information about the topic we discussed today?
- Join my workshop on (date), and experience my framework first-hand.
- Scan the QR code in the handout to access my free speaking resource (or newsletter), and let me know if you find it helpful.
- It has been a pleasure to have you as a guest on our podcast. We'd love to invite you back to the show!
- Subscribe to my YouTube channel and ring the bell to get reminders when I post new training videos and pro tips.
- Sign up for my Three-Day Challenge to Confidence (any challenge as it relates to the subject matter).
- For all attendees who joined the seminar today, email me a recording of your un-pitch for personalized feedback.
- Connect with me on LinkedIn, and weigh in on the conversation.
- Text me for Part Two of the webinar series. There's more to unpack from what we covered today in Part One.

There will be times when you won't be able to cover everything or answer all the questions in the time you're given to present. Let your audience know that you are listening to what they're asking, you'll look into it, and you'll get back to them. This is permission for you to follow up with a second point of contact and takes the pressure off you having to cram your speech full of too much information.

As social creatures, they crave connection. They want to click. That's not to say that when people experience reciprocity they will act on it right away. They may not; however, they will remember how they felt at that moment when you gave them something.

I've coached a lot of doctors, lawyers, financial experts, policy makers, entrepreneurs, designers, and other professionals. They all convert their clients on trust. People want to know you and trust you before you ask them to invest in your new widget, go forward with a business relationship, or even get married! All are big commitments.

> Trust is fundamental, reciprocal, and pervasive.
> If it is present, anything is possible.
> If it is absent, nothing is possible.
>
> —George P. Schultz

Reciprocity can secure a second meeting. In the next subchapter, I'll lay out ways for you to facilitate meetings that are a great experience for everyone.

Meetings Makeover

Love meetings? Is that even possible? I know there are so many meetings vying for your attention—the VP of finance wants the quarterly reports, the senior manager wants a status update on the new project, the client wants to brainstorm solutions with the creative team—that it can seem like your professional life is meeting after meeting after meeting. I've even referenced meetings over twenty times in this book!

Meetings are inevitable for doing business; however, based on the following statistics compiled by Zippia,[52] meetings are costing companies staggering amounts of time and money.

- An estimated thirty-seven billion dollars and twenty-one billion hours are lost per year to unproductive meetings.
- The average corporate employee spends four hours preparing for and attending meetings per week.
- Sixty-five percent of employees agree that meetings prevent them from completing their own work.

It doesn't help that public speaking skills are rarely taught on the job, and yet they're expected for all levels of employees in order to do the job well. Whether in meetings, presentations, emails, collaborations, or online forums, effective communication is a cornerstone of success in virtually every profession. So many daily interactions depend on speaking that investing in speaking skills for all staff should be a no-brainer.

I've never met anyone who said they wish they could attend more meetings, but there are times when they are necessary. So what can you do to make meetings an effective use of everyone's time as well as a great experience?

First and foremost, using the Remarkable Framework will save you and your team hours of meeting preparation. Second, it will help you get crystal clear about your goals and objectives. Having a clear direction will ensure the meeting is productive with enough space for participants to make contributions. Third, with the tools of the Framework, you can reduce the running time and potentially the number of meetings everyone needs to attend.

As a speaker, your opening is to facilitate the meeting and guide the conversation. Encourage communication between attendees by incorporating interactive elements to spark participation and raise the energy of the room. For example, use this variation of the Tree Grid and have people list ideas to resolve an issue with sixty-second writing sprints at different stages of the meeting.

TREE GRID WORKSHEET	
Section D **Call to Action** What action is a possible solution for the problem?	
Section B **What Is The Supporting Content?** What moments, experiences, examples, anecdotes, data, case studies, industry news, and so on best explain the problem in Section A?	**Section C** **Why Share This Content?** For each piece of content listed in Section B, write why it is important to share. What is the lesson learned or what value does this have for solving the problem?
1B	1C
2B	2C
3B	3C
Section A **Big Idea** What is the problem we are trying to solve?	

I'm sure you've been in plenty of meetings where people don't say how they really feel. There's usually hesitation and awkward silences. It's almost like the work you're doing here on speaking training is at the root of what they're going through. Always come back to the book. Here is how you can use the Framework to create that safe space that I discussed in Chapter 3 because when you care, they care.

Use the icebreakers I introduced in Chapter 2 to set a familiar tone, inviting people into the conversation.

Refer to Chapter 4, and facilitate the Hand Off technique and interjecting. You'll ensure everyone gets a chance to contribute and keep the discussion moving forward. Listen actively to switch from a lecture to a value-driven interaction.

Motivate and empower your team by writing variations of the I AM statement described in Chapter 5. When you promote others, you acknowledge their work, and they gain mutual respect from colleagues. Try something like this:

My coworker ____________ is good at ____________ because they succeeded at ____________.

For example:
My coworker *Theo* is good at *closing the deal with prospects* because they succeeded at *presenting interactive demonstrations that make it a great experience*.

If you scheduled a thirty-minute meeting, reserve five minutes at the end for a Q&A. Ask open-ended questions, allowing people to give some thought to their responses instead of a simple *yes* or *no*. "What brought you to that conclusion?" and "How can I better support the team to meet the deadline?"

Whether the focus of your meeting is on status updates, decision making, problem solving, team building, or innovation, wrap things up with a call to action like I talked about in the previous subchapter. These are engaging ways to extend the conversation and inspire collaboration.

Don't Be an Influencer, Be Influential

> I've had rainbows in my clouds. And the right thing to do, it seems to me, is to prepare yourself so that you can be a rainbow in somebody else's cloud.
>
> —Maya Angelou

Think of the moment when a mentor showed up in your life. The details may be a little fuzzy, but you likely remember that moment, and it has probably influenced you to this day. With the speaking skills you've developed throughout this book, it's your turn to inspire others by sharing your experiences and moving people beyond your words. It's time to become the rainbow in somebody else's story.

In Chapter 5, I talked about the value of reflecting on moments and how they reveal so much about you and your journey. Your stories are not the fleeting sound bites of an influencer. Your stories can have an impact on someone, a long-lasting memory that makes you influential.

When interviewed on the World Economic Forum's "Meet the Leader" podcast, primatologist and anthropologist Jane Goodall told a story about her chance encounter with a taxi driver who criticized her work and his own sister's work because both focused on animals instead of people.[53]

On that trip to the airport in London, Goodall explained, "I told him stories about the chimps, how we were helping people to rise out of poverty." When they reached their destination, the driver didn't have the correct change, so she told him to donate the extra to his sister for her work. Weeks later, Goodall received a letter from the driver's sister, thanking her for both the donation and sparking her brother's genuine interest in animals. Goodall understood: "You've got to reach the heart. It's no good arguing with the head. It's no good blinding someone with statistics."

Your goal is not to impress anybody. You can't try to make somebody like you or control how others feel. You can, however, talk about your experiences and their significance to you. When you're influential, you have a more profound and lasting effect on people and you can shape industries and cultures. Those who align with what you're saying may embrace their work more because they feel they're part of a bigger mission.

You may influence people as a subject-matter expert when they ask you to be a guest on their podcast or a featured panelist or keynote speaker. They will appreciate your stories of wisdom and see you as a role model for others.

I never searched for a mentor; they always seemed to arrive like a rainbow. They showed up at times in my life when I needed tutelage and encouragement. It was usually something they said or did, and we just clicked.

It appears to be that way with my mentees as well. Something I said or did, leveraging my experiences as a costume designer or as the founder of Big Idea consultancy and Remarkable Speaking, have all allowed me to show up for others.

> A teacher affects eternity; he can never tell where his influence stops.
>
> —Henry Brooks Adams

I'm encouraging you to continue seeking those opportunities to talk about your stories. When you enter a room, be curious about people and what's around you. When you ask more questions than you deliver answers, you make the room smarter and inspire leaders at every level.

Flip to page 182 in Chapter 10 and write your takeaways for leveraging your message. Now is the time to experience what it means to embody Remarkable Speaking.

CHAPTER 10 EMBODY

The Experience

Congratulations! You're now speaking up in places you only once imagined you would. You're doing it!

Let's take a step back in time to a moment that happened last year or the day before you picked up this book.

Reflect on your speaking skills at that moment.

Reflect on that meeting when you were nervous and too inhibited to speak up.

Reflect on that day when your self-talk was so loud that you felt that your every word was being judged.

Reflect on that presentation when you struggled to get your words out because your heart was pounding out of your chest.

Now give yourself grace and compassion for the speaker that you are today.

Today, you reframe your thoughts and get out of your head. Today, you ask questions and make meetings and presentations a great experience for others. Today, you share information through conversation and move the world with your words.

Using the Remarkable Framework, you're speaking up more, interacting more, and even recording videos! You're talking about your experiences, and people see you for the leader you are.

Embody this moment. Time is giving you perspective.

In the past, you longed for the time when you could speak confidently. Looking into the future then, you wanted to speed up time, pushing to get a desired outcome. You are now in the present and savoring time.

Whatever your professional status or personal lifestyle, your speaking and communication has reached another level.

No matter how many times you reread and reference the pages of this book, you will continue to discover new moments to add to your story bank. With every sprint, you will see each experience from a different perspective and notice something that you hadn't noticed before.

I am truly honored that you put your trust in me to guide you on your speaking journey. It may have felt like I pushed you to do things that were uncomfortable and even a little scary. But it was a push from a good place in my heart because I know what you're capable of. You like a challenge and creating new experiences—those of a remarkable speaker!

Read on to see how those experiences reflect on your presence in an executive manner of speaking.

Be the Speaker You Want to Hear

One of the most dreaded questions my clients struggle with is: "Tell me about yourself." Another struggle I hear about is the expectation that they should be charismatic and have an executive presence like Steve Jobs.

There's no doubt when Jobs spoke that people really connected with his X factor. Even the naysayers were captivated. But you're not Steve Jobs, and his legacy is taken.

So be yourself, and let people experience you. They will experience your X factor, which is the aura of executive presence.

> Be yourself; everyone else is already taken.
>
> —Oscar Wilde

Executive presence doesn't mean you have to talk in the most intellectual or the most comprehensive way. By speaking in your own words, you share your journey, you lead by example, and you build your own legacy. Remember, when you embody your voice and your vision equally, you can change the world.

> If your actions create a legacy that inspires others to dream more, learn more, do more, and become more, then, you are an excellent leader.
>
> —Dolly Parton

In the 1960s, Mary Quant defined women's fashion, creating looks known as the "Swinging Sixties" and the "Chelsea Look."[54] Quant believed clothing should be relaxed and comfortable, reflecting the modern-day lifestyle. Her whimsical, vibrantly colored mini skirts and hot pants presented a stark contrast to the rigid structure of Parisian couturiers that dominated society at the time, representing a new generation of trailblazing women.

Quant's legacy was about relaxed clothes that reflected everyday life. Your legacy about your experiences also reflect everyday life.

When you felt good about your talk, then other people felt good about it too. This is authenticity.

When you shared your experiences, you took your listeners on your journey with you. This is transcendence.

When you took a deep breath and created space, then you spoke with executive presence. This is ownership.

I often think about how confidence translates throughout life. There isn't a weekend you and a weekday you. You are the same person everywhere you show up.

"Tell me about yourself" is your opportunity to share a moment from your journey. People want to hear what you have to say, and it will encourage you to go further.

You are remarkable in all aspects of your life, and you look forward to speaking with purpose and excitement. This is confidence.

The R.E.M.A.R.K.A.B.L.E. Framework

I am here for you, but, unfortunately, I'm not going to be in the room when you give your next speech, nudging you to breathe or share your stories. So keep coming back to the book. With the Remarkable Framework and the following speaking resources (your key takeaways and speaker survival checklist) on hand, it will feel like I'm right there with you.

Following are the key takeaways you wrote at the conclusion of each chapter. If you've written all nine chapters of your takeaways, then you are one chapter away from having your personalized speaking survival guide! Your takeaways are to reinforce what you've learned, strengthen those neural pathways, and motivate you to keep speaking.

CHAPTER 1: **R**EFRAME

Get out of your head.

CHAPTER 2: **E**MPOWER

Take ownership of what you believe.

CHAPTER 3: MIC-DROP MOMENT

Let your emotions transcend your words.

CHAPTER 4: ACTIVATE

Step into the spotlight!

CHAPTER 5: REFLECT AND REVEAL

Explore self-expression.

CHAPTER 6: KEEP QUIET

Give silence a voice.

CHAPTER 7: ARTICULATE

Clarify and bring your big idea to life.

CHAPTER 8: BE THE BRIDGE, NOT THE BARRIER

Have conversations that connect.

CHAPTER 9: **L**EVERAGE YOUR MESSAGE

Transfer your skills for excellence.

CHAPTER 10: **E**MBODY

Manifest confidence and speak remarkably.

The Framework is your gateway to confidence. It's permission to continue your journey. It's permission to learn. It's permission to explore. It's permission to make mistakes. It's permission to enjoy the process. It's permission to have your voice and be seen.

Giving myself permission to explore reminds me of the time when I traveled through Italy, and the owner of a local trattoria asked me how I was enjoying my visit. I told him it was a fun challenge to walk across as many bridges as possible in Venice. I said I will never forget relaxing in the ancient termes in the hills of Tuscany or the experience of learning about making wine and olive oil while spending time at a friend's vineyard. But there was so much more that I wanted to experience.

With a smile, he said something that has influenced me to this day: "Enjoy this moment, and know you'll always have something to come back to."

Always come back to the book.

Your Speaking Survival Checklist

Along with your key takeaways, I've created a speaking survival checklist.

Checking the boxes on the list before your next talk will give you a sense of accomplishment and confidence. It will help you stay focused on what's important so you can be more productive as a speaker.

When you're motivated to learn more, subscribe to my social channels on the Connect page on my website, remarkablespeaking.com. It is a one-stop to stay up to date on new releases and never miss a pro tip. You'll get access to my speaking how-tos, informational videos, upcoming speaking events, workshops, and more.

Check the list, then let go and talk about what you know.

- ☐ Every opportunity to speak is an opportunity to have a conversation.
- ☐ If you're feeling nervous, reframe that thought to "I am excited!"
- ☐ If someone says they had a good day, be curious and ask them what made it good.
- ☐ Take a breath. The breath gives you space, separating turbulence from clarity.
- ☐ If you want to warm up, do some Power Up drills and speak up.

- ☐ If you feel doubtful, own your thoughts with "I believe."
- ☐ If the audience looks too big, have conversations and engage in a few icebreakers before things kick off.
- ☐ If you make a mistake, turn it into a relatable commonality by making it part of the conversation.
- ☐ If you feel uncomfortable, do it again so it will become more familiar.
- ☐ If you're caught up with too many technical cues, repeat a few tongue twisters and get out of your head.
- ☐ If you want to create a buzz with your speaking, record a video to reply to an email or text.
- ☐ If someone is hogging the conversation, interject and hand off to the group to make it a great experience.
- ☐ When you give your introduction, share a mic-drop moment and stand out from the crowd.
- ☐ If you catch yourself summarizing, use a speaking prompt with "I," "me," or "my" language to get to a real moment.
- ☐ If you feel like you're speaking too fast, manage your energy with a few breaths to slow down.
- ☐ When you find yourself rambling and trailing off topic, use a speaking prompt; you'll come back much stronger.
- ☐ If you're struggling to connect with your big idea, use the Shelley Grinder to eliminate extraneous details and articulate your words.
- ☐ If you're at a loss for words, tap into your story bank and talk about what you know.
- ☐ If you're pressed for time writing the outline for your talk, sprint to save time.
- ☐ If the circumstances for your talk change, revisit the Evergreen to edit and adapt.

With these resources and the Remarkable Framework, you'll continue to transition the drills from these pages into speaking in the real world.

Your speaking will be less about a transaction and more of a profound connection, and that's remarkable!

What Makes You Remarkable?

Dolce far niente! An Italian saying that translates to "the sweetness of doing nothing." The intention of this adage is not meant to be lazy; it's a reminder to take the time to smell the roses.

As a speaker, take the time to observe everything that's around you in the room. Think of it as if it were a garden. There are roses and other flowers. You hear birds chirping, see children playing, and hear water trickling from a stream. The garden is more than just flowers taking root. Similarly, you're talking to more than just a room full of people.

Speaking excellence is something that you've wanted for a long time, and with all the hard work you've done up to this point in the book, you're ready. You're more than ready.

You're having conversations and gaining new perspectives, personally and professionally, and bringing those experiences to life.

You are crystal clear about your purpose, and it's leading you to wonderful things.

You know it won't be perfect, but with ownership, you don't see setbacks.

With the Remarkable Framework, you not only speak more confidently, but you are more confident.

You created the space. Feel that energy in your body and soul, and say it out loud: "I am remarkable!"

You've embodied your voice and your vision equally. You now understand what it means to be a remarkable speaker.

Confidence looks good on you.

I look forward to seeing you on that stage.

As always, speak remarkably!

A NOTE FROM ME TO YOU

I like to think of our time together as the road not taken. Whatever road you choose, the opportunities are boundless. This is your hero's journey.

Thinking of you, my first client comes to mind. She was so nervous when she had to speak because she really, really wanted her speeches to be great.

She was anxious and talked really fast. She felt the unbelievable pressure of perfection, especially when sharing her thoughts with an audience. She envied other speakers who appeared confident and at ease.

Today, she has worked with over a thousand people across five continents as a captivating speaker. She continues to use the Framework and speaks up even if she has nothing to say.

But at times, she still gets nervous.

She learned to embody her voice and speak what's on her mind and do so in her own words. When she gave herself permission to let go of old beliefs, remarkable conversations started to happen.

That first client is me.

My wish for you is to continue to enjoy speaking because the world's a better place when you have conversations that connect. As a remarkable and confident speaker, people understand what kind of business person you are; they know what kind of leader you are and what kind of friend you are.

It is my honor and a privilege, as your coach, to have shared this journey with you.

ENDNOTES

1 "Unconscious decisions in the brain." *Max-Planck-Gesellschaft*, 14 Apr. 2008, mpg.de/research/unconscious-decisions-in-the-brain.

2 Cloke, Harry. "The Science Behind Curiosity in Learning." *Growth Engineering*, 10 May 2023, growthengineering.co.uk/what-is-curiosity.

3 Chandler, Steve. *Shift Your Mind Shift the World.* 2nd ed., Maurice Bassett, 2018.

4 Kratochvil, Renate, and Bjoern Schmeisser. "How Will You Measure Your Life?, by Clayton M. Christensen, James Allworth, and Karen Dillon." *Academy of Management Learning & Education*, Book & Resource Reviews, vol. 20, no. 1, 2021, pp. 112–15, doi.org/10.5465/amle.2020.0148.

5 Gladwell, Malcolm. *Outliers: The Story of Success.* Little, Brown and Company, 2008.

6 Lally, Phillippa, et al. "How are habits formed: Modeling habit formation in the real world." *European Journal of Social Psychology*, vol. 40, 2010, pp. 998–1009, onlinelibrary.wiley.com/doi/10.1002/ejsp.674.

7 Clear, James. *Atomic Habits: An Easy & Proven Way to Build Good Habits & Break Bad Ones.* Avery, 2018.

8 Sinek, Simon. *Start with Why: How Great Leaders Inspire Everyone to Take Action.* Portfolio, 2009.

9 Benabou, Roland, and Jean Tirole. "Self-Confidence and Social Interactions." *National Bureau of Economic Research*, Working Paper 7585, Mar. 2000, doi.org/10.3386/w7585.

10 Mlodinow, Leonard. *Emotional: The New Thinking About Feelings.* Allen Lane, 2022.

11 "The Most Popular TED Talks of All Time." *TED*, ted.com/playlists/171/the_most_popular_ted_talks_of_all_time. Accessed 19 Sept. 2024.

12 Izard, Carroll. "Emotion Theory and Research: Highlights, Unanswered Questions, and Emerging Issues." *Annual Review of Psychology*, vol. 60, no. 1, 2009, pp. 1–25, doi.org/10.1146/annurev.psych.60.110707.163539.

13 Semeraro, Alfonso, et al. "PyPlutchik: Visualising and comparing emotion-annotated corpora," PLoS ONE, vol. 16, no. 9, 1 Sept. 2021, doi.org/10.1371/journal.pone.0256503.

14 Galvez-Pol, Alejandro, et al. "Emotional representations of space vary as a function of peoples' affect and interoceptive sensibility." *Scientific Reports*, vol. 11, 2021, 16150, doi.org/10.1038/s41598-021-95081-9.

15 Paul, Annie Murphy. *The Extended Mind: The Power of Thinking Outside the Brain*. Mariner, 2022, p. 69.

16 Hoffman, Reid, et al. *The Alliance: Managing Talent in the Networked Age*. Harvard Business Review Press, 2014.

17 Future of StoryTelling. "Q&A with Professor of Neuroscience Uri Hasson." *Medium*, 10 Jan. 2020, medium.com/future-of-storytelling/q-a-with-professor-of-neuroscience-uri-hasson-b57e23476fab.

18 Ibid.

19 Chang, Rachel. "How Mahalia Jackson Sparked Martin Luther King Jr.'s 'I Have a Dream' Speech." *Biography*, 29 Mar. 2021, biography.com/musicians/mahalia-jackson-i-have-a-dream-influence.

20 Future of StoryTelling. "Q&A with Professor of Neuroscience Uri Hasson." *Medium*, 10 Jan. 2020, medium.com/future-of-storytelling/q-a-with-professor-of-neuroscience-uri-hasson-b57e23476fab.

21 Unknown illustrator. "From the Tee: Too Many Swing Thoughts." *Lake Magazine*, 26 May 2016, lakemagazine.life/lakemartinliving/golf/from-the-tee-too-many-swing-thoughts/article_71ceddb1-5178-565e-beb6-09142980d0bf.html.

22 Gurr, Alanna. "The Top Video Marketing and Sales Stats that Matter." *Vidyard*, 14 July 2023, vidyard.com/blog/sales-and-marketing-stats.

23 Ruan, Sherry, et al. "Comparing Speech and Keyboard Text Entry for Short Messages in Two Languages on Touchscreen Phones." *Proceedings of the ACM on Interactive, Mobile, Wearable and Ubiquitous Technologies*, vol. 1, no. 4, 2018, pp. 1–23, doi.org/10.1145/3161187.

24 Newburger, Eric. "Home Computers and Internet Use in the United States: August 2000." *U.S. Census Bureau Current Population Reports*, Sept. 2001, census.gov/content/dam/Census/library/publications/2001/demo/p23-207.pdf.

25 Caro, Robert. *The Path to Power (The Years of Lyndon Johnson, Volume 1).* Vintage, 1990.

26 Saldana, Sean. "Turning every page: Exploring the relationship between Robert Caro and Robert Gottlieb." *The Texas Standard,* TPR, 31 Jan. 2023, tpr.org/arts-culture/2023-01-31/turning-every-page-exploring-the-relationship-between-robert-caro-and-robert-gottlieb.

27 Suttie, Jill. "Why We Should Share Our Good News (Not Just Our Struggles)." *Greater Good Magazine,* 23 Jan. 2024, greatergood.berkeley.edu/article/item/why_we_should_share_our_good_news_not_just_our_struggles?

28 Ibid.

29 museumoffailure.com.

30 "History Timeline: Post-it® Notes." *Post-it® Brand,* post-it.com/3M/en_US/post-it/contact-us/about-us. Accessed 19 Sept. 2024.

31 "Durable Skills." *America Succeeds,* 2021, americasucceeds.org/policy-priorities/durable-skills. Accessed 23 July 2024.

32 Dyvik, Einar. "Number of employees worldwide from 1991 to 2024." *Statista,* 4 July 2024, statista.com/statistics/1258612/global-employment-figures.

33 MacLaren, Neil, et al. "Testing the babble hypothesis: Speaking time predicts leader emergence in small groups." *The Leadership Quarterly,* vol. 31, no. 5, 2020, 101409, doi.org/10.1016/j.leaqua.2020.101409.

34 "Karen Lynch." *World Economic Forum,* weforum.org/people/karen-lynch. Accessed 20 Sept. 2024.

35 Gillespie, Lane. "Survey: 48% of social media users have impulsively purchased a product seen on social media." *Bankrate,* 18 Sept. 2023, bankrate.com/personal-finance/social-media-survey.

36 "Apollo 13: Mission Details." *NASA,* 26 July 2023, nasa.gov/missions/apollo/apollo-13-mission-details. Accessed 20 Sept. 2024.

37 Knapp, Jake, et al. *Sprint: How to Solve Big Problems and Test New Ideas in Just Five Days.* Simon & Schuster, 2016.

38 Parkinson, C. Northcote. "Parkinson's Law." *The Economist,* 19 Nov. 1955, economist.com/news/1955/11/19/parkinsons-law.

39 "History of Advertising No 85: The 'I heart New York' logo." *Campaign*, 21 Nov. 2013, campaignlive.co.uk/article/history-advertising-no-85-i-heart-new-york-logo/1221536.

40 Umejima, Keita, et al. "Paper Notebooks vs. Mobile Devices: Brain Activation Differences During Memory Retrieval." *Frontiers in Behavioral Neuroscience*, vol. 15:634158, 2021, doi.org/10.3389/fnbeh.2021.634158.

41 López Lloreda, Claudia. "Handwriting may boost brain connections more than typing does." *Science News*, 26 Jan. 2024, sciencenews.org/article/handwriting-brain-connections-learning.

42 "Vilfredo Pareto." *New World Encyclopedia*, newworldencyclopedia.org/entry/Vilfredo_Pareto. Accessed 20 Sept. 2024.

43 Grant, Adam. *Hidden Potential: The Science of Achieving Greater Things*. Viking, 2023.

44 Maybin, Simon. "Busting the attention span myth." *BBC World Service*, 10 Mar. 2017, bbc.com/news/health-38896790.

45 Shank, Patti. "Attention and the 8-Second Attention Span." *eLearning Industry*, 4 Apr. 2017, elearningindustry.com/8-second-attention-span-organizational-learning.

46 Ibid.

47 Murre, Jaap, and Joeri Dros. "Replication and Analysis of Ebbinghaus' Forgetting Curve." *PLoS ONE*, vol. 10, no. 7: e0120644, 2015, doi.org/10.1371/journal.pone.0120644.

48 Madore, Kevin, and Anthony Wagner. "Multicosts of Multitasking." *Cerebrum: the Dana forum on brain science*, vol. 2019 cer-04-19, 2019, ncbi.nlm.nih.gov/pmc/articles/PMC7075496.

49 "Read My Pins: The Madeleine Albright Collection," *National Museum of American Diplomacy*, readmypins.state.gov/see-the-pins. Accessed 20 Sept. 2024.

50 "Elisha Otis." *PBS: They Made America*, pbs.org/wgbh/theymadeamerica/whomade/otis_hi.html. Accessed 20 Sept. 2024.

51 Strohmetz, David B., et al. "Sweetening the Till: The Use of Candy to Increase Restaurant Tipping." *Journal of Applied Social Psychology*, vol. 32, 2006, pp. 300–309, doi.org/10.1111/j.1559-1816.2002.tb00216.x.

52 Flynn, Jack. "28+ Incredible Meeting Statistics [2023]: Virtual, Zoom, In-Person Meetings and Productivity." *Zippia*, 6 July 2023, zippia.com/advice/meeting-statistics.

53 Lacina, Linda, host. "Turning points and lessons learned: Meet The Leader's top leadership moments so far." *Meet the Leader*, World Economic Forum, 10 Nov. 2023, weforum.org/podcasts/meet-the-leader/episodes/best-leadership-moments-so-far.

54 "Introducing Mary Quant." *Victoria and Albert Museum*, vam.ac.uk/articles/introducing-mary-quant. Accessed 20 Sept. 2024.

ABOUT THE AUTHOR

Shelley Goldstein studied at the Fashion Institute of Technology in New York and Boston University's School of Fine Arts for theatrical design. She cut her teeth as a costume designer working for shows on Broadway, at the New York City Opera, and in Ringling Bros. and Barnum & Bailey Circus.

An opportunity to design for MGM's Pink Panther License led Shelley to work with the studio's graphics department, where she went from hand-drawing storyboards to digitizing them. Fascinated with the burgeoning computer arts industry, she learned the tools of digital media and launched Big Idea, a full-service marketing consultancy, in 1998. Her client roster spanned the environmental, fashion, sports, hospitality, and entertainment industries.

In 2002, Shelley went in-house for a sporting goods client, developing their marketing department over fifteen years of growth while pioneering their digital marketing at the dawn of the internet marketing era.

In 2020, Shelley became a certified Ultraspeaking coach, and, in 2022, she founded Remarkable Speaking as a keynote speaker, public speaking coach, and corporate trainer. With over thirty years of senior-level management, entrepreneurship, marketing, and design expertise, Shelley has coached more than one thousand individuals from over forty-seven countries on five continents and across a wide variety of industries to develop the skills necessary to become confident, remarkable speakers.

Storytelling has been a common thread of Shelley's career journey starting with clothing for revealing the character's story, to messaging for telling the brand's story, to coaching for amplifying the voice for all speakers to express their vision and captivate their audiences.

As a passionate advocate for social justice, Shelley is committed to creating a more equitable world. She donates her time to disadvantaged individuals to build their confidence to help them to use their voices to champion for themselves and their communities.

To connect with Shelley and join her in conversation, visit:

linkedin.com/in/shelleygoldstein
remarkablespeaking.com.

TESTIMONIALS

I was very, very excited to hear that Shelley Goldstein was going to publish a book because I've seen her speak, and I've seen her help a lot of speakers around the world.

Shelley is special because she really believes. She believes that everybody can become a powerful communicator; that everybody can change the world by communicating; that everybody has a skill; that everybody has potential. She understands that each and every single talent is unique and special and valuable.

Shelley embodies that belief in the way she teaches, in the way she interacts with people. Her message got people at my international organization really motivated and moved. Shelley is able to see a person's potential, see their bottlenecks, see the fear or the lack of confidence they're feeling, and then offer them the resources and tools to overcome those challenges. They wind up really feeling confident becoming themselves, unleashing their true potential.

I'm so excited that Shelley is going to spread this know-how and magic to the world through *Remarkable Speaking* so that everybody feels more confident being themselves and goes on to change the world.

Tomoo Okubo
External Affairs Officer, World Bank Group

I always appreciate Shelley's advice on the power of storytelling to connect with an audience in an authentic way. I learned from her that no audience can know or appreciate any speaker's perspective or genius unless that speaker shares their emotions in a truthful and genuine way. Everything that she and Gary Vaynerchuk have encouraged me to do more of has enabled me to lay my own foundation for standing out and connecting!

Seema Alexander
Cofounder & President, Virgent AI
Founder, Disruptive CEO Advisory
Creator, U.N.I.Q.U.E. Method™

As a tech entrepreneur and consultant, speaking in front of a room and building relationships was never an enjoyable experience for me. The amount of anxiety I would have over preparation would drain me. Shelley's Remarkable Framework taught me how to be more relaxed, more present, and find my own voice—especially with my one-on-one interactions with clients. I sought out to become a better speaker, and I also learned how to become a better listener.

Aaron Winaker
Owner, Home Helpers Home Care
Former Managing Partner, Applico

As a former VP at Morgan Stanley on Wall Street, I communicated through the traditional rigid approach to public speaking—that whoever talks the most will dominate the conversation. But working with Shelley has completely revolutionized the way I communicate. By utilizing her Remarkable Framework, I have become a more skilled speaker *and* a more powerful and impactful human being. Shelley's coaching goes beyond tips and tricks—she zeroes in on the hidden blocks holding me back and helps me break through them in a way that feels both profound and permanent. Now, whether I'm in line at the grocery store or pitching a large corporate client, I'm fully present and engaged, communicating from a place of authenticity.

Shelley refuses to let me settle for surface-level presentation styles often found in typical "how-to-present" books. Whenever I start playing small or glossing over the real story, she calls me out, pushing me to get deep, lead with openness, and speak with conviction. From that place, everything else—voice, pacing, confidence—just flows. It feels effortless.

Shelley also equips me with quick-to-use techniques for those moments when old habits sneak back in. I can now naturally pause, pivot, recenter, and start a dialogue in a way that feels second nature. Above all, Shelley has made me fall in love with my own message and given me the tools to share it boldly and authentically. Her book, *Remarkable Speaking*, distills all of her wisdom into one dynamite package. If you've ever wished to truly connect with an audience and speak with impact, this is the book you need in your hands. You won't regret it.

Susan Chen
Vedic Meditation Teacher
Founder, Meditate with Susan

www.ingramcontent.com/pod-product-compliance
Lightning Source LLC
Chambersburg PA
CBHW051306120626
46547CB00015B/2115

* 9 7 8 1 9 5 6 8 3 7 4 1 4 *